family recipes

a collection of delicious family recipes

Contents

This edition published in 2010 by L&K Designs. Text by Sara Porter.
© L&K Designs 2010
PRINTED IN CHINA

Publishers Disclaimer

Whilst every effort has been made to ensure that the information contained is correct, the publisher cannot be held responsible for any errors and or omissions. Please note certain recipes may contain nuts or nut oil.

Short of Culinary Inspiration?

Do you find yourself racking your brains on a daily basis, trying to figure out what to put in lunchboxes or what to cook your family for dinner? Are you feeling a little bit like a one-trick-pony when it comes to creating interesting family meal ideas? Do you stare into your fridge and food cupboards, willing them to give you some much-needed inspiration? Or do you simply dread family gatherings or the in-laws coming to dinner because they've already seen all your best culinary-moves? Well, if you're longing for some really delicious, nourishing and stress-free recipes, then look no further because help is here! It's time to put the joy back into your cooking!

Family Recipes is packed with recipes for adults and children to enjoy. Including yummy breakfast/brunch recipes, tasty lunchbox and picnic ideas, seasonal food favourites, fabulous 'celebration' foods and hearty family meals.

No More TV Dinners!

We seem to have lost the meaning of the good old-fashioned family value of eating dinner together around a table, having all-but disappeared amongst ever-increasing frantic work schedules, readymade dinners, children hypnotised by computer or gaming screens whilst picking at their food, (I suppose we should be encouraged by their ability to multi-task!), teenagers not wanting to ruin their 'street-cred' by having dinner with the rest of the family and nights glued to the box with TV dinners on our laps.

And it's such a shame! We lose a valuable opportunity for our families to catch up with one another at the end of each day, sharing our experiences and interacting as a family, whilst enjoying great food. Family Recipes provides a wide range of tempting, family oriented meal ideas that aim to encourage everyone in getting back around the table – keeping the whole family happy, healthy and brimming with energy and life!

Breakfast

Breakfast

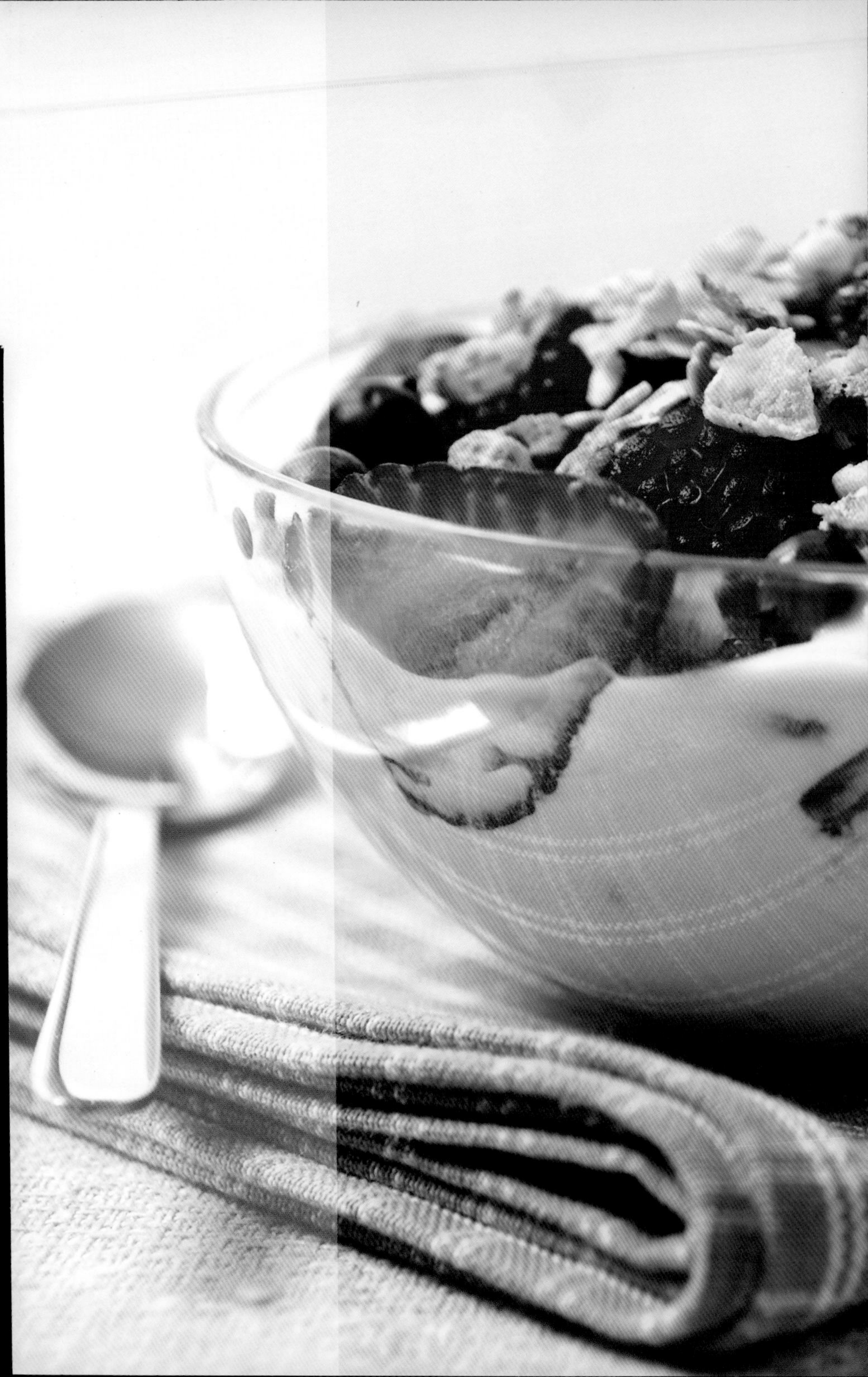

Blueberry Bread (Serves 4-6)

Ingredients

225g/1 1/2 cups fresh blueberries
200g/1 3/4 cups of plain flour
150g/2/3 cup of sugar
2 eggs (large)
115ml/1/2 cup of milk
112g/1/2 cup of butter (unsalted)
1 tbsp grated lemon zest
1/2 tsp vanilla extract
1 tsp baking powder
1/4 tsp salt

Method

1. Preheat the oven to 180C/350F/Gas mark 4. Spray the inside of a 9 x 5 x 3 inch loaf pan with non-stick cooking spray; or lightly grease with butter.

2. Place the flour, salt and baking powder in a bowl and mix together well. Place the butter, (slightly warmed), in a large bowl and beat with a hand-blender for about 1 minute. Add the sugar and beat until the mixture is light and fluffy.

3. Add the eggs, one at a time, and beat the mixture thoroughly after each new addition. Add the lemon zest and vanilla extract and beat well.

4. Add 1/3 of the flour, mixing with the blender on low continuously. Follow this by adding 1/2 of the milk, still mixing continuously. Repeat this process alternately until all the flour and milk are mixed in – ending with the flour.

5. Fold in the blueberries, gently distributing them as evenly as possible. Transfer the mixture into the loaf pan and place in the center of the oven for 55-60 minutes, until golden brown.

6. Remove from the oven and leave to cool for 5 minutes. Turn out onto a wire cooling rack to cool completely.

Creamed Mushroom Bagels (Serves 4)

Ingredients
4 plain bagels (halved)
400g/4 cups of mushrooms (sliced)
12 tbsps soured cream
110g/1/2 cup of butter
3 tbsps fresh dill (chopped)
1 shallot (finely chopped)
3-4 tsps lemon juice

Method
1. Melt the butter in a small pan and add the chopped shallots, cook over a gentle heat for 4-5 minutes, until tender.

2. Add the mushrooms and increase the heat a little. Cook for 4-5 minutes, until the mushrooms begin to brown. Add the lemon juice and cook for 1 minute. Remove from the heat.

3. Toast the bagels and butter. Stir the soured cream and dill into the mushroom mixture and then spoon over the bagel halves.

Egg & Mushroom Scramble (Serves 4)

Ingredients
100g/1 cup of Cheddar cheese (grated)
250g/2 1/2 cups of fresh mushrooms (halved)
7 eggs
2 tbsps milk
2 large tomatoes (sliced)
30g/1/8 cup of butter
2 tbsps parsley (chopped)

Method
1. Lightly grease a 600ml (1 pint), ovenproof dish. Heat the butter in a large frying pan and add the halved mushrooms. Cook for 4-5 minutes, until softened and lightly browned.

2. Remove from the heat and transfer the mushrooms into the ovenproof dish. Place the eggs in a bowl and beat together with the milk and parsley.

3. Pour the egg liquid into the frying pan and scramble over a medium heat, until the egg is set. Preheat the grill to a medium heat.

4. Spoon the eggs over the mushrooms and top with the tomato slices. Sprinkle over the top with cheese. Place under the grill and brown for a couple of minutes. Remove from the heat and serve immediately.

Eggy-Bread with Bacon (Serves 2-4)

Ingredients
4 slices thick white bread (preferably crusty)
8 rashers of streaky bacon
6 eggs
3 tbsps milk
1 tbsp vegetable oil
salt & black pepper (to season)
Maple syrup (to serve)

Method
1. Preheat the grill to a medium/high heat. Place the eggs and milk in a mixing jug and season with salt and black pepper; beat together well. Pour into a shallow bowl.

2. Heat half of the vegetable oil in a non-stick frying pan over a medium heat. Place two slices of the bread in the egg mixture and add to the heated frying pan.

3. Cook for 5-6 minutes until golden, turning halfway through cooking. Remove from the pan and keep warm. Repeat the process for the remaining two slices of bread.

4. Whilst the eggy-bread is cooking, cook the bacon under the preheated grill for 5-6 minutes, until crispy. To serve, slice each eggy-bread in half, diagonally and top with two slices of bacon. Drizzle with maple syrup and serve immediately.

Fresh Fruit Salad & Granola Cereal (Serves 4)

Ingredients

60g/1/2 cup of granola cereal
125g/1/2 cup of yoghurt
1/2 apple (diced)
1/2 pear (diced)
1 banana (sliced)
2 peeled oranges (cut into segments)
250g/2 cups of halved red grapes
2 tbsps of fresh orange juice
1 tbsp of raisins

Method

1. Add all the fruit ingredients to bowl, (including the orange juice), and mix together.

2. Sprinkle the granola mixture over the top and mix gently. Divide the mixture equally into 4 bowls and top with yoghurt.

Hash Browns (Serves 4)

Ingredients
500g/2 cups of peeled & cooked potatoes (diced)
1 medium onion (finely chopped)
4 tbsps vegetable oil
salt & black pepper (to season)

Method
1. Heat the oil in a large frying pan and add the potatoes, forming a single layer of potato chunks. Sprinkle the onion over the top and season with salt and black pepper.

2. Cook over a medium heat, until golden brown underneath, regularly pressing the potatoes down with a spatula or the back of a wooden spoon.

3. Once browned underneath, cut the hash into quarters and turn each over using a fish slice. Cook again, until golden brown and heated through. Serve immediately.

Chorizo, Egg & Potato Brunch (Serves 4)

Ingredients
500g/2 cups of salad potatoes (scrubbed & thickly sliced)
250g/2 1/2 cups chorizo sausage (skinned & sliced)
4 eggs
bunch of spring onions (sliced)
1 1/2 tbsp olive oil

Method
1. Cook the potatoes for 4-5 minutes. Drain, return to the pan and stir in the olive oil. Heat a frying pan and add the potatoes. Cook for 7-8 minutes, until golden brown.

2. Heat a large, separate frying pan and add the chorizo sausage and spring onions. Cook for 3-4 minutes. Add the potatoes and toss all the ingredients together.

3. Whilst the sausage and spring onions are frying, poach the eggs in boiling water. Transfer the potato mixture to 4 individual serving dishes and top each with a poached egg.

Orange Marmalade Breakfast Muffins (Makes 12)

Ingredients
115g/1/3 cup thick-cut orange marmalade
200g/1 3/4 cups of plain flour
55g/1/2 cup of wholemeal flour
170ml/3/4 cup of semi-skimmed milk
110g/1/2 cup of butter (melted)
75g/1/3 cup of unrefined caster sugar
1 large egg
1 orange, juice and zest
1 tbsp baking powder
pinch of salt

Method
1. Preheat the oven to 200C/400F/Gas mark 6. Line a muffin tray with 12 muffin cases.

2. Sift the baking powder, plain flour and salt into a bowl. Add the caster sugar and wholemeal flour and stir in well.

3. Place the melted butter, egg, milk, orange juice and zest in a bowl and mix together. Gradually mix into the flour mixture, alternating with mixing in the orange marmalade.

4. Spoon the mixture into the muffin cases to about 2/3 full, giving them room to rise. Place in the oven for 20-25 minutes, until golden and risen. Remove from the oven and leave to cool a little. Best served warm.

Smoked Salmon & Scrambled Eggs (Serves 4)

Ingredients
4 eggs
8 egg whites
55g/1/4 cup of smoked salmon (cut into thin strips)
black pepper (to season)
fresh dill, or chopped chives

Method
1. Place the eggs and egg whites in a bowl and whisk together. Add black pepper to season, according to taste.

2. Spray a large non-stick frying pan with low-fat cooking spray and heat over a low/medium heat. Add the eggs and gently cook them until curds begin to form.

3. Using a spatula or a wooden spoon, move the eggs around so that the uncooked parts cook. Keep doing this for 1-2 minutes until the eggs are almost set.

4. Stir in the salmon and fresh dill and mix in well. Remove from the heat and serve with a slice of wholewheat toast.

Spiced French Toast (Makes 6 Slices)

Ingredients
6 slices of bread
2 large eggs
110ml/1/2 cup of milk
1/2 tsp ground cinnamon
1/2 tsp ground nutmeg
1 1/2 tsp light brown sugar (soft)

Method
1. Lightly oil a frying pan. Place the eggs in a large bowl and beat together. Add the sugar, nutmeg and milk and combine well.

2. Dip the bread slices into the mixture, covering them equally. Heat the oil over a medium heat and add the dipped bread slices, cook both sides, until lightly browned.

3. Remove from the pan and place on serving plates. Sprinkle with a little cinnamon and serve.

Picnics
&
Pack-ups

Picnics & Pack-ups

BLT Sandwich Stacks (Makes 24)

Ingredients
18 slices square bread (white or wholemeal)
24 thin cucumber slices
375g/1 2/3 cups of soft cheese
12 rashers of back bacon
4 tomatoes (sliced)
iceberg lettuce leaves
cocktail sticks (optional)

Method
1. Preheat the grill to a medium/high setting and grill the bacon, until just crispy, (8-10 minutes). Leave to cool for 2-3 minutes.

2. Toast the bread to just golden and cut off the crusts. Place to one side. Place the soft cheese in a bowl and mix to soften a little more. Spread over the top of 12 slices of lightly toasted bread.

3. Top 6 of the slices of bread with tomato, cucumber and lettuce, followed by a plain slice of toast on each.

4. Place 2 rashers of the cooked bacon on top of each plain slice, (on the top of the stack), followed by the remaining cheese spread toast, (spread side-down).

5. Cut each sandwich into 4 triangles and either serve immediately, or wrap with cling wrap, refrigerate and serve when ready.

For a more party-like feel, decorate the ends of cocktail sticks with tinsel, mini-paper flags, or other decorations and push them into each side of the sandwich, about 2-3cm from each corner, before cutting.

Cheese, Celery & Apple Sandwich (Serves 4)

Ingredients
8 slices of wholemeal bread
50g/1/2 cup of cheddar cheese (grated)
100g/1 cup of gruyere cheese (grated)
55g/1/4 cup of mayonnaise
2 celery sticks (finely chopped)
2 apples (cored & grated)
handful of cress
butter (to spread)

Method
1. Place both cheeses in a bowl and combine well. Mix in the grated apple, mayonnaise, chopped celery and cress.

2. Spread the bread with butter and fill the sandwiches with the mixture. Serve immediately.

Chicken Salad Pockets (Makes 6)

Ingredients
250g/2 cups of cooked chicken breast (diced)
1/4 of an iceberg lettuce (shredded)
6 wholemeal pitta breads
175g/1 cup of seedless green grapes (halved)
1/2 stick of celery (finely chopped)
50g/1/2 cup of mozzarella cheese (grated)
salad dressing

Method
1. Place the chicken, grapes, celery and cheese in a bowl and add your preferred salad dressing. Gently toss the ingredients together.

2. Cut the pitta bread and open into pockets and equally fill with lettuce. Spoon in the chicken mixture and serve.

Chocolate Cornflake Cakes (Makes 12)

Ingredients

90g/3 1/2 cups of cornflakes
115g/4 oz dark chocolate (broken into pieces)
4 tbsps golden syrup
40g/2/3 cup of butter

Method

1. Place the chocolate, butter and golden syrup in a saucepan and gently heat, stirring continuously. Blend the mixture together well.

2. Stir in the cornflakes, coating them well. Spoon a heaped tablespoon of the mixture into paper cake cases and place on a tray. Place in the refrigerator for at least 1 hour, until the cakes have set.

Cranberry & Citrus Punch (Makes approx. 2 Litres)

Ingredients

1 ltr/4 1/2 cups of lemon & lime soda water
785ml/3 1/2 cups of fresh orange juice
1/2 ltr/2 cups cranberry juice

Method

1. Place the ingredients in a large jug and mix together well. Transfer to a pitcher and serve over ice.

Creamy Picnic Coleslaw (Serves 4)

Ingredients

1/2 head of green cabbage (finely shredded)
1 large carrot (finely shredded)
1 tbsp white vinegar
1 tbsp grated mild onion
110g/1/2 cup of mayonnaise
1 tbsp sour cream
1 tbsp dry mustard
3/4 - 1 tbsp sugar (to taste)
1 tsp celery salt
salt & black pepper (to season)

Creamy Picnic Coleslaw/cont.

Method

1. Place the shredded cabbage and carrot in a large bowl and mix together.

2. Place the sour cream, mayonnaise, onion, sugar, mustard, celery salt and vinegar in a bowl and season with salt and black pepper. Mix together well.

3. Add the creamy mixture to the cabbage/carrot mixture and toss together well. Taste and adjust the seasoning/sugar if desired. Transfer to a serving bowl, cover and refrigerate.

Crudités with Humous Dip (Serves 4-6)

750g vegetable crudités, such as; carrot batons, broccoli florets, sliced pepper strips, baby sweetcorn, celery sticks, chicory leaves, etc – to be served on large plates, with dips in the centre.

Humous Dip

Ingredients

800g/3 1/3 cups canned chickpeas (drained & rinsed)
395ml/1 3/4 cups of tahini
4 cloves of garlic (crushed)
16 tbsps water
6 tbsps lemon juice
4 tsps ground cumin
2 tbsps extra virgin olive oil
3 tsps paprika
1/2 tsp salt

Method

1. Place the chickpeas, garlic, cumin, lemon juice, tahini, salt and water in a food processor and blend until creamy.

2. Spoon out into a serving bowl and smooth over with the back of a spoon. Drizzle with olive oil and sprinkle over paprika.

Deli Beef Pittas (Serves 4)

Ingredients

500g/3 1/3 cups of roast beef slices
2 avocados (peeled & cubed)
4 pitta breads (cut in half)
2 spring onions (finely chopped)
4 tbsps apple cider vinegar
1/2 tbsp Dijon mustard
60ml/1/4 cup of olive oil
salt & black pepper (to season)

Method

1. Place the vinegar, olive oil and Dijon mustard in a bowl and mix together. Season with a little salt and black pepper and whisk together.

2. Add the roast beef slices, avocado cubes and the chopped spring onions and toss gently, coating the ingredients. Fill each of the pockets with the filling and serve.

Ham & Cheese Wheels (Makes 12)

Ingredients

50g/1/3 cup of cooked ham
50g/1 cup of carrot (grated)
2 slices large wholemeal bread (crusts removed)
55g/1/4 cup of soft cream cheese
margarine (for spreading)

Method

1. Flatten the bread with a rolling pin and spread with a small amount of margarine.

2. Place the grated carrot and soft cream cheese in a bowl and mix together. Spread over the bread.

3. Top each slice of bread with ham and then roll the bread up. Cut into 6 'wheels' and skewer each with a cocktail stick.

Homemade Mini Sausage Rolls (Makes 24-28)

Ingredients
500g pork sausages (skins removed & chopped)
2 sheets of frozen puff pastry (defrosted, but still chilled)
2 eggs (beaten)
75ml/1/3 cup of milk (maybe a little more)
1/2 onion (finely chopped)
25g/1/2 cup of fresh white breadcrumbs
2 tbsps flour

Method
1. Line 2 trays with baking paper. Place the milk and breadcrumbs in a bowl and leave for 5-10 minutes, until the breadcrumbs have absorbed the milk.

2. Place the chopped onion, 1 egg, sausagemeat and soaked breadcrumbs in a food processor and blend until all the ingredients are well combined. Transfer to a bowl, cover and refrigerate for 30-40 minutes.

3. Sprinkle flour over a clean work surface and place one of the sheets of pastry on top. Make a horizontal cut across the pastry, cutting it into 2 pieces.

4. Carefully spoon 1/4 of the sausagemeat mixture, in a line, along the centre of each pastry piece.

5. Fold over one of the long sides of the pastry sheet and brush with the other beaten egg. Fold over the other side of the pastry, overlapping a little in the centre – making a sausage shape. Repeat this process with the rest of the pastry and sausagemeat filling, (making 2 rolls in total).

6. Place the 4 rolls onto the baking trays, seam side downwards. Cover and chill in the refrigerator for 30-40 minutes.

7. Preheat the oven to 180C/350F/Gas mark 4. Line 2 baking trays with non-stick baking paper. Diagonally cut the rolls into 6 or 7 pieces and brush with the remaining egg; make 2 small slits in the top of each roll with a sharp knife.

8. Transfer the sausage rolls to the fresh baking trays and place in the oven for 25-30 minutes, until the pastry has risen and the rolls are golden brown. Remove from the oven and leave to cool a little for 5 minutes before serving.

Mini-Quiches (Makes 8)
Ingredients
2 slices of thick ham (diced)
375g/5 cups of spinach (washed)
5 large eggs
110ml/1/2 cup of milk
3 cherry tomatoes (halved)
2 tbsps fresh Parmesan cheese (grated)
2 tbsps chives (finely chopped)
 extra tbsp fresh Parmesan cheese (grated)
black pepper (to season)

Method

1. Place the spinach in a non-stick frying pan and cook over a high heat, tossing it constantly, until wilted. Remove from the heat and leave to cool. Remove from the pan and squeeze dry. Set to one side.

2. Preheat the oven to 180C/350F/Gas mark 4. Using baking paper, cut out 8 x 6 inch squares and use to line a deep muffin tray.

3. Place the eggs, 2 tablespoons of Parmesan cheese, milk and chives in a bowl; season with black pepper. Beat the ingredients together.

4. Equally distribute the spinach and ham into the paper muffin moulds. Spoon in the egg mixture and top with two cherry tomato halves in each one.

5. Place in the oven for 13-15 minutes, until set. Remove from the oven and top with the extra Parmesan cheese. Leave to cool a little before serving. Serve hot or cold.

Mozzarella & Tomato Bites (Makes 20)

Ingredients
10 small mozzarella balls
20 cherry tomatoes
20 basil leaves (washed & dried)
1/4 tsp salt

Method
1. Halve the mozzarella balls
and place in a bowl; season
with salt.

2. Skewer each of the halves
onto a cocktail stick; adding 1 basil
leaf and 1 cherry tomato on each.
Cover and refrigerate for 1 hour before serving.

Pink Lemonade (Makes 3 Litres)

Ingredients
450ml/2 cups of fresh lemon juice
1.8 litres/8 cups of water
280g/1 1/4 cups of caster sugar
4 tsps grenadine
12 maraschino cherries
2 cups of ice

Method
1. Place the lemon juice, ice, sugar, grenadine and water in a food processor and blend until smooth.

2. Place a cherry in the base of each glass and pour in the pink lemonade. Serve immediately!

Potato Salad (Serves 4-6)

Ingredients
700g/4 cups of salad potatoes (scrubbed)
6-8 rashers of smoked streaky bacon (chopped)
1 large onion (chopped)
4 tbsps mayonnaise
4 tbsps Spanish mayonnaise
black pepper (to season)

Method
1. Boil the salad potatoes, as per packet instructions. Fry the bacon in a frying pan for 4-5 minutes, until cooked. Remove and set aside.

2. Add the onions to the frying pan and cook for 3-4 minutes in the bacon fat. Remove with a slotted spoon and set aside.

3. Drain the cooked potatoes and transfer them to a large bowl, add the mayonnaise and toss well, coating the potatoes well. Add the Spanish mayonnaise and toss well again, coating the potatoes.

4. Add the onions and bacon. Gently toss together, combining ingredients well. Season with black pepper, according to taste. Serve warm or cold.

Scotch Eggs (Makes 6)

Ingredients
6 large hardboiled eggs (shelled, rinsed & dried)
470g/1 lb sausagemeat
135g/1 1/2 cups of dry white breadcrumbs
1 large egg (beaten)
2 1/2 tbsps plain flour (seasoned with salt & black pepper)
black pepper (to season)
vegetable oil (for frying)

Method
1. Knead some black pepper into the sausagemeat and divide into 12 equal sized pieces. Take two pieces of the sausagemeat and flatten them.

2. Place a little flour on a plate and roll one of the cooked eggs in the flour. Gently brace the egg between the two portions of meat and carefully mould around the egg; sealing the halves together evenly and leaving no holes.

3. Repeat this process with the remaining sausagemeat and eggs. Place the seasoned flour on a plate, place the beaten egg in a bowl and the breadcrumbs on another plate. Line the three ingredients up, in their respective orders – the breadcrumbs being nearest to your cooking hob.

4. Pour between 4-5cm of vegetable oil into the saucepan and heat for about 1 minute. Roll each of the eggs, one at a time; firstly in the seasoned flour, then dip in the beaten egg and finally coat with breadcrumbs. Fry in the oil for 7-10 minutes, until golden brown.

5. Drain on absorbent kitchen paper and leave to cool. Repeat this process for the remaining eggs.

Summer Fruits with Mint (Serves 4)

Ingredients

250g/1 1/4 cups of fresh strawberries (quartered)
175g/1 cup of seedless green grapes (halved)
1/2 ripe cantaloupe melon (cubed)
75g/1/3 cup of sugar
280ml/1 1/4 cups of dry white wine (optional)
1 tbsp fresh mint leaves (chopped)

Method

1. Place the wine and sugar in a saucepan and bring to a gentle boil; cook for 2 minutes, stirring until the sugar dissolves. Remove from the heat and leave to cool a little.

2. Place the grapes, melon, strawberries and mint in a bowl and gently toss together. Pour the warm wine/sugar mixture over the fruit mixture and gently toss again.

3. Cover and refrigerate for 2-3 hours, taking the mixture out and stirring it occasionally. Serve when ready.

Summer Strawberry Sandwiches (Serves 4)

Ingredients

250g/1 1/4 cups of strawberries (sliced)
2 tbsps caster sugar
8 slices of large, crusty white bread
55g/1/4 cup of unsalted butter

Method

1. Spread the bread with the butter and arrange the strawberry slices on 4 of the slices of bread.

2. Sprinkle the strawberries with a little caster sugar and top with the remaining bread. Cut into quarters and serve.

Tuna & Apple Sandwiches (Serves 4)

Ingredients
225g/1 cup of canned tuna (drained)
8 large, thick slices of wholemeal bread
1 apple (cored & finely chopped)
110g/1/2 cup of soft cheese
2 spring onions (finely chopped)
1 tbsp lemon juice

Method
1. Spread the bread with soft cheese. Place the apple in a bowl and add the lemon juice. Toss well. Add the tuna and spring onions and mix the ingredients together well.

2. Top 4 slices of the bread with the mixture and top with the remaining bread. Slice into diagonal halves and serve.

After
School

After School

Chicken Pitta with Yoghurt (Serves 4)

Ingredients
4 chicken breast fillets
4 pitta breads
100g/2/3 cup of cucumber (chopped)
110g/1 1/2 cups of mixed salad leaves
330ml/1 1/3 cups of natural yoghurt
2 cloves of garlic (crushed)
juice of 1/2 lemon
2 tsps clear honey
1 tsp ground cumin
salt & black pepper (to season)

Method
1. Pour 110ml of the yoghurt into a bowl; add half the cumin and season with salt and black pepper. Combine well.

2. Slice the chicken breasts into 5 slices and place in the mixture, coating each slice well. Cover and refrigerate for 2-3 hours.

3. Preheat the grill to a medium heat and grill the chicken slices for 8-10 minutes, until golden brown, (turning halfway). Remove from the grill and leave to cool for 5 minutes.

4. Place the remaining yoghurt, lemon juice, garlic, cumin and honey in a bowl. Season with salt and black pepper, according to taste.

5. Warm and split the pitta breads and equally divide the salad and cucumber and place inside. Fill each with chicken and spoon over the top with the yoghurt dressing. Serve immediately.

Corn on the Cob (Serves 4)

Ingredients
4 corn on the cob (husks & silk removed)
60g/1/4 cup of butter
salt & black pepper (to season)

Method
1. Place the corn on the cob in a large frying pan and cover with boiling water. Boil gently for 3-5 minutes, turning once.

2. Drain the corn on the cob and transfer to a large dish. Cover evenly with butter and season with salt and black pepper, according to taste.

Chocolate Banana Lollies (Makes 4)

Ingredients
2 bananas
8 chunks of plain cooking chocolate
desiccated coconut
4 lolly sticks

Method
1. Peel and halve the bananas crossways. Place a lolly stick in each banana half. Cover a medium-sized plate with desiccated coconut.

2. Break the cooking chocolate in a bowl and place in a saucepan of simmering water. Heat until the chocolate has melted. Pour out into a shallow dish, leave to cool a little.

3. Roll the banana pieces in the chocolate and then in the desiccated coconut. Place directly onto a baking tray and freeze for 2 hours.

To serve, remove from the freezer 15 minutes before eating.

Fruit Tortilla Wraps (Serves 4)

Ingredients
4 flour tortillas
2 bananas (chopped)
4 large strawberries (chopped)

2 nectarines (chopped)
2 tsps runny honey

Method
1. Spoon the fruit in a line down the centre of each tortilla and drizzle with a little honey. Roll the tortillas up, folding in the ends.

2. Heat a non-stick frying pan and place the wraps, seam-side down, in the pan. Cook for 4 minutes, turning the wraps over halfway through cooking.

3. Remove from the pan and serve warm.

Healthy Apple Crisps! (Serves 4)
Ingredients
4 crunchy apples (such as Golden Delicious)
110g/1/2 cup of sugar
juice of 1 lemon
110ml/1/2 cup of water

Method
1. Preheat the oven to 150C/300F/Gas mark 2. Place the sugar, lemon juice and water in a saucepan and heat gently, dissolving the sugar.

2. Bring to the boil for 1 minute and then remove from the heat. Leave to cool.

3. Cut the top and bottom from the apples and slice them as thinly as possible; giving you thin 'discs'.

4. Dip the discs in the cooled syrup and place directly onto a baking tray. Place in the oven to cook for 1 hour.

5. Turn off the oven and leave the apple in the oven overnight. Remove the next morning and you should have perfect crisps!

Healthy Fruit & Nut Bars (Makes approx. 12)

Ingredients

140g/1 1/4 cups of porridge oats
110g/1/2 cup unsalted butter
55g/1/4 cup of demerara sugar
40g/1/4 cup of dried apricots (finely chopped)
40g/1/4 cup of sultanas
40g/1/4 cup of dried figs (chopped)
50g/1/4 cup of pecan nut halves
40g/1/4 cup of dried dates (chopped)
2 1/2 tbsps honey
30g/1/4 cup of walnuts (crushed)
1 3/4 tbsps apricot conserve
25g/1/4 cup of dried cranberries
1 tbsp pumpkin seeds
1 tbsp shaved coconut
1/2 tbsp sunflower seeds
1/2 tbsp pistachio nuts (chopped)

Method

1. These delicious and nutritious bars can be made in advance as they will keep well in an airtight tin or container. Preheat the oven to 190C/375F/Gas mark 5. Line a square cake tin with baking paper.

2. Melt the butter in a saucepan and add the demerara sugar, honey and apricot conserve. Cook, and stir for 1-2 minutes, until the sugar dissolves.

3. Bring to the boil and cook for a further couple of minutes, stirring continuously, so as not to burn. Remove from the heat.

4. Add the remaining ingredients to the saucepan, mixing all the ingredients together well.

5. Transfer the mixture to the cake tin and spread it out evenly. Place in the oven for 18-20 minutes, until golden.

6. Remove from the oven and leave to cool for 10-15 minutes. Score the 'cake' into bar shapes and remove from the cake tin to cool completely.

Naan Bread Dippers (Serves 4-6)

Ingredients

4-6 naan breads (cut into strips)
1 tbsp lemon juice
1/2 cucumber (grated)
500g/2 cups of Greek yoghurt
1 1/2-2 handfuls of fresh coriander leaves
handful of fresh mint leaves
3 tbsps olive oil
paprika (to season)
salt (to season)

Method

1. Place the grated cucumber in a bowl and squeeze out as much juice as you can, using your hands. Remove the juice, leaving the grated cucumber.

2. Place the mint and coriander leaves and Greek yoghurt in a food processor and blend until well combined. Transfer to a dish.

3. Stir the cucumber into the mixture; mixing together well. Cover and refrigerate for at least 20 minutes.

4. Preheat the oven to 180C/350F/Gas mark 4. Lay the naan strips on baking trays and brush the top-side with the olive oil. Sprinkle over the top with salt and paprika.

5. Place in the oven for 7-10 minutes, until crisp and lightly browned. Remove from the oven and leave to cool for 1-2 minutes. Add the lemon juice to the Raita and serve with the naan dippers.

Pizza Dippers

Ingredients
1 ready-made pizza dough
8oz/1 cup jar of Bolognese sauce
1 tbsp olive oil
oregano
garlic salt

Method
1. Preheat the oven to 180F/350F/Gas mark 5. Lightly grease a baking tray.

2. Cut the pizza dough into 1 inch by 6 inch strips. Place the strips about 1/2 inch apart on the baking tray. Brush with olive oil and season with garlic salt and oregano, according to taste.

3. Place in the oven for 12-15 minutes, until golden brown. Heat the sauce and pour into a serving bowl. Dip the pizza sticks in the sauce and eat!

Potato & Chickpea Bites (Serves 4-6)

Ingredients
600g/2 1/2 cups canned chickpeas (drained & rinsed)
3 potatoes (peeled & diced)
1 1/2 onions (finely chopped)
1 fresh green chilli (finely sliced)
2 tomatoes (sliced)
2 tsps chilli powder
9 tbsps water
3 tbsps tamarind paste
3 tsps sugar
1 tsp salt

Method
1. Place the chickpeas in a large bowl and leave to one side. Boil the diced potatoes in a pan of boiling water for 6-10 minutes, until tender. Drain and leave to one side.

2. Place the tamarind paste and water in bowl and mix together. Add the sugar, chilli powder and salt and mix well. Pour over the chickpeas.

3. Add the diced potatoes and onion and gently mix all the ingredients together, combining them well.

4. Transfer to 6 small serving bowls and top with the sliced tomatoes and fresh chilli.

Spicy Mixed Nuts (Serves 4)

Ingredients
115g/3/4 cup of roasted peanuts
115g/3/4 cup of pistachio nuts
115g/3/4 cup of cashew nuts
2 tsps garam masala
2 tbsps vegetable oil

Method
1. Place all of the nuts in a bowl and add the garam masala; mix together well, coating the nuts with the spice.

2. Heat the vegetable oil in a frying pan and add the nut mixture. Cook, moving the nuts around the pan constantly, for 2-3 minutes, until lightly browned. Remove from the pan and leave to cool before serving.

Bacon & Feta Cheese Omelette (Serves 4)

Ingredients
180g/1 1/2 cups of feta cheese (crumbled)
2 tbsps crème fraiche
6-8 large eggs (beaten)
4-6 rashers of cooked bacon (chopped)
2 cooked potatoes (chopped into small pieces)
1 small onion (finely chopped)
60g/1/4 cup of butter
2-3 tbsps olive oil

Bacon & Feta Cheese Omelette/cont.

Method

1. Preheat the grill to a medium setting. Heat the butter and olive oil in a non-stick frying pan and add the onion and bacon. Cook for 2-3 minutes, until very lightly browned.

2. Add the chopped potato and cook for 2-3 minutes, until lightly browned. Place the eggs and crème fraiche in a mixing jug and whisk together. Pour over the potato/bacon mixture in the frying pan and sprinkle over the top with the crumbled feta cheese.

3. Cook in the frying pan until the egg begins to set. Remove from the heat and place under the grill to cook the centre/top of the omelette. Keep under the grill until golden brown. Serve immediately with a side salad.

Beef & Beer Supper (Serves 2-4)

Ingredients

650-700g/ 1 3/4 lbs canned, stewed steak (in gravy)
6-8 slices of French bread (one side toasted)
3-4 tbsps beer
1/2 tbsp brandy
1/2 tbsp wholegrain mustard
1-2 tbsps instant mashed potato powder
1 tbsp butter

Method

1. Place the stewed steak, brandy and beer in a saucepan and heat through for 3-4 minutes, stirring occasionally.

2. Sprinkle the instant potato powder over the top and stir well, thickening the sauce. Cook for 1-2 minutes. Transfer the mixture into an ovenproof casserole dish and preheat the grill to a medium/high heat.

3. Place the butter and mustard in a small dish and mix together. Spread evenly over the un-toasted sides of the French bread. Lay on top of the meat mixture, buttered side-up. Place under the grill for 3-4 minutes, until toasted. Serve immediately.

Beef & Pepper Noodles (Serves 4)

Ingredients

500g/2 cups of beef fillet (cut into thin strips)
1 red pepper (sliced)
1 green pepper (sliced)
1 onion (sliced)
1 clove of garlic (crushed)
1 inch piece of root ginger (finely chopped)
2 tbsps lemon juice
2-3 tbsps vegetable oil
fresh egg noodles
salt & black pepper (to season)

Method

1. Preheat a wok and add the oil. Once the oil has heated,
add the garlic and stir-fry for 1-2 minutes. Add the beef strips
and cook for 2-3 minutes, until lightly browned. Stir in the ginger and then
remove the wok from the heat.

2. Remove the beef from the wok with a slotted spoon and keep to one
side. Return the wok to the heat and add the peppers and onion. Stir-fry
over a high heat for 3-4 minutes. Heat the noodles, as per the packet
instructions, approximately 3-4 minutes.

3. Return the beef to the wok and stir in the lemon juice. Season with salt
and black pepper, according to taste. Serve over the cooked noodles.

Bubble & Squeak (Serves 4)

Ingredients

450g/2 cups potatoes (peeled & boiled)
50g/1/2 cup of chopped bacon
125g/1 cup of cabbage or Brussel sprouts (cooked and shredded)
55g/1/4 cup of butter
1 tbsp chopped parsley
2 tbsps vegetable oil
pinch of black pepper

Bubble & Squeak/cont.

Method

1. Once the potatoes have been boiled, drain and add in the butter and black pepper. Mash the potatoes.

2. Fry the chopped bacon until crispy and then stir into the mash. Add in the cabbage or sprouts, along with the parsley. Shape the mix into 4 balls and flatten down to about 2 inch-high cakes.

3. Heat the oil in a frying pan and fry each of the cakes for 3-4 minutes on each side – until golden brown. Serve with a side salad.

Butternut Squash Risotto (Serves 4)

Ingredients

450g/2 cups of long-grain rice
1 butternut squash (peeled & cubed)
2 courgettes (chopped)
1 red pepper (deseeded & chopped)
1 onion
150g/1 cup of frozen peas
1 litre vegetable stock
30g/1/8 cup of butter
1 tbsp vegetable oil
1/4 tsp ground turmeric

Method

1. Heat the butter and vegetable oil in a large saucepan and add the onion and turmeric. Cook for 3-4 minutes, until just tender.

2. Add the vegetable stock and rice and bring to the boil. Reduce the heat, cover and simmer for 15 minutes.

3. Whilst the rice is cooking, boil the butternut squash cubes for 7-9 minutes or until just tender - and cook the peas for 3-4 minutes. Drain each and add to the rice mixture.

4. Stir in the courgettes and red pepper and cook for about 5 minutes, until heated through. Serve immediately.

Cheese, Onion & Bean Hot Pot (Serves 4)

Ingredients
150g/1 1/2 cups of grated cheese
100g/2 cups of cooked macaroni
190g/3 cups of canned kidney beans (drained & rinsed)
8 tomatoes (peeled & finely chopped)
1 onion (cut into rings)
2 cloves of garlic (crushed)
2 red peppers (cut into rings)
1/2 cup of tomato puree
1 tsp chilli powder
2 tbsps butter
salt & black pepper (to season)

Method
1. Preheat the oven to 200C/400F/Gas mark 6. Grease a large baking dish with butter. Heat the butter in a pan and add the onion. Cook for 3-4 minutes, until tender. Add the peppers and cook for 1 minute.

2. Add the garlic, chilli powder and tomatoes and cook for 4-5 minutes, stirring continuously. Stir in the kidney beans, pasta and tomato puree. Season with salt and black pepper and mix together well.

3. Transfer the mixture to the baking dish and sprinkle over the top with cheese. Place in the oven and cook for 20 minutes. Serve immediately.

Cheesy Beans! (Serves 4-6)

Ingredients
155g/1 1/4 cups of cheddar cheese (cut into chunks)
560g/9 cups of canned kidney beans (drained & rinsed)
600g/8 cups of canned butter beans (drained & rinsed)
185g/1 1/2 cups of button mushrooms
4 tomatoes (quartered)

Cheesy Beans!/cont.

1 onion (sliced)
1 green pepper (chopped)
1 1/2 tbsps tomato puree
3 tbsps Worcestershire sauce
1 tbsp vegetable oil

Method
1. Heat the oil in a frying pan and add the onions and pepper. Cook for 4-5 minutes, until tender.

2. Add the beans, mushrooms, tomato puree and Worcestershire sauce. Cook for 6-8 minutes on a low-medium heat, stirring regularly.

3. Add the tomatoes and cheese chunks. Cook for a few minutes, until the cheese is partially melted. Remove from the heat. Serve with warm crusty bread.

Cheesy Vegetables on Toast (Serves 4)

Ingredients
8 slices of bread
4-6 mushrooms (thinly sliced)
2 tomatoes (thinly sliced)
1 red pepper (thinly sliced)
14-16 thick slices of mature Cheddar cheese
1 tsp minced garlic (optional)
black pepper (to season)
dash of Tabasco sauce
butter (for spreading)

Method
1. Preheat the grill to a medium setting. Toast the bread, until lightly golden brown. Spread the toast with a little butter and spread the minced garlic evenly over each slice.

2. Layer the slices of mushrooms, peppers and tomatoes on each slice of toast and top with 2 slices of cheese, per piece.

3. Place under the grill for 2-3 minutes, until the cheese has melted. Remove from the grill and season with black pepper. Add a dash of Tabasco sauce to give it an extra kick! Serve immediately.

Chicken & Broccoli Stir-Fry (Serves 4)

Ingredients
4 chicken breasts (skinless and cubed)
450g/2 cups of broccoli florets
450g/2 cups of shredded cabbage
210g/2 cups of brown rice (cooked)
170g/3/4 cup of frozen peas
75ml/1/3 cup of orange juice
1 tbsp olive oil
1 tbsp soy sauce
1 tbsp schezuan sauce
2 tsps cornstarch
1 tbsp sesame seed

Method
1. Begin by cooking the brown rice, as per the packet cooking times. Whilst the rice is cooking, place the soy sauce, orange juice, schezuan sauce and cornstarch in a bowl and mix together.

2. Heat the olive oil in a wok and add the chicken. Stir-fry for about 7-8 minutes and then add in the vegetables and sauce mixture. Stir-fry for about 5-7 minutes until the vegetables are properly heated.

3. Drain the brown rice and arrange on serving plates. Serve the stir-fry over the brown rice and top with a sprinkle of sesame seeds.

Corned Beef & Potato Hash (Serves 4)

Ingredients
700g/4 cups of potatoes (cubed)
350g/12 1/2 oz canned, corned beef (diced)
180g/6 1/2 oz canned, sweetcorn (drained)
1 onion (chopped)
1 red pepper (diced)
2 tsps Worcestershire sauce

Corned Beef & Potato Hash/cont.

2 tbsps vegetable oil
1 tbsp fresh parsley (chopped)
salt & black pepper (to season)

Method

1. Boil the potatoes for 12-15 minutes, until tender. Drain and set to one side. Heat the oil in a frying pan and add the potatoes and sauté for 8-10 minutes, until golden brown.

2. Add the red pepper and onion and cook for 5-6 minutes. Remove from the heat. Add the sweetcorn, corned beef and Worcestershire sauce. Season with salt and black pepper, according to taste.

3. Return to the heat and cook for 8-10 minutes, until heated through. Serve immediately, sprinkled with a little chopped parsley.

Creamy Fettuccini with Salmon (Serves 4)

Ingredients

335g/1 1/2 cups of cooked salmon (skinned & boneless)
75g/1 cup of mushrooms (sliced)
250g/2 1/2 cups of fettuccine pasta
150g/3/4 cup of tomatoes (chopped)
225ml/1 cup of single cream
2 tbsps butter
2 tbsps chopped onions
1 tbsp flour
75g/1/2 cup of frozen peas (thawed)
1/4 tsp oregano
1/4 tsp basil
1/2 tbsp fresh parsley (chopped)
salt & black pepper (to season)

Method

1. Cook the pasta, as per the packet instructions. Heat the butter in a large frying pan and add the onions and mushrooms. Cook for 4-5 minutes, stirring frequently.

2. Stir in the flour until well mixed, followed by the cream. Bring to the boil; reduce the heat and simmer, stirring continuously, for 1-2 minutes.

3. Add the peas, salmon, oregano, basil, parsley and tomato and season with salt and black pepper. Cook for 3-4 minutes, stirring occasionally.

4. Drain the cooked fettuccine and return to the pan. Pour in the salmon mixture and gently combine. Serve immediately.

Fish Curry (Serves 4)

Ingredients
450g/1 lb haddock (skinless & chopped)
300ml/1 1/3 cups of fish stock
75g/1/2 cup of creamed coconut
30g/1/8 cup of butter
20g/1/8 cup of sultanas
1 small onion (finely chopped)
2 tbsps sweet chutney
1 tbsp plain flour
1 tbsp curry powder
1 clove of garlic (crushed)
2 tsps tomato puree
juice & grated rind of 1/2 lemon

NB. Cooking times are based on an 800W microwave oven.

Method
1. Place the butter in a casserole dish on high power for 20-30 seconds, until melted. Stir in the haddock, onion and garlic and cover the dish. Cook on high for 3 minutes.

2. Stir in the curry powder, lemon juice and rind, flour and fish stock. Re-cover and cook on high for 3 minutes, stirring midway through cooking. Then stir in the sultanas, chutney and tomato puree, re-cover and cook for 3-4 minutes, stirring occasionally.

3. Break the coconut up with a fork and stir into the cooked curry. Stand for 4-5 minutes. Serve over a bed of hot rice.

Grilled Salmon & Swiss Cheese Toasty (Serves 4)

Ingredients
100g/1 cup of grated Swiss cheese
225g/8oz canned salmon (skinless, boneless & drained)
8 slices of whole grain bread
1/3 cup of mayonnaise
40g/1 1/2oz grated carrots (ready-grated)
1 spring onion (chopped)

Method
1. Place the salmon, Swiss cheese, mayonnaise, spring onions and grated carrot in a bowl and gently mix together.

2. Equally divide the mixture and place between two slices of bread. Butter the outsides of the bread and place in a toasty-maker, (or a dual contact grill), for 4-5 minutes.

Homemade Vegetable Pizza (Serves 4)

Ingredients
2 ready made pizza bases (10-12 inch)
1 red pepper (finely chopped)
1 green pepper (finely chopped)
440g/3 1/2 cups of sliced mushrooms
110g/4oz canned sweetcorn (drained)
2 225g/8oz cans of chopped tomatoes
2 tbsps tomato puree
350g-400g/3 1/2-4 cups of grated mozzarella cheese
1-2 cloves of garlic, (crushed)
pinch of oregano
black pepper

Method
1. Preheat the oven to 190C/375F/Gas mark 5. Place the tinned tomatoes into a bowl and mix in the tomato puree, crushed garlic, oregano and black pepper. Spread the mix equally on each pizza base.

2. Sprinkle the grated cheese over each pizza base and top with the vegetables.

3. Place in the oven directly on the shelf, one on the middle shelf and one above, swapping them around halfway through cooking. Remove from the oven after about 20 minutes and cut into equal slices.

Hot Beef & Potato Supper (Serves 4)

Ingredients
450g/3 cups of rump or sirloin steak (cut into 1 inch long strips)
620ml/2 3/4 cups of beef stock (hot)
340g/1 1/2 cups of cooked new potatoes (halved)
140g/2/3 cup of cherry tomatoes (halved)
1-2 cloves of garlic (crushed)
60g/1/2 cup of plain flour
1-2 red onions (sliced)
2 tsps paprika
1 tbsp fresh chives (chopped)
1 tbsp vegetable oil
1 tbsp Worcestershire sauce
salt & black pepper (to season)

1. Place the flour in a bowl and add the paprika, mix together well. Toss the strips of beef in the mixture, coating them well and place to one side.

2. Heat the vegetable oil in a large frying pan and add the coated beef strips. Cook for 3-4 minutes, stirring occasionally to brown all sides of the meat.

3. Add the garlic, potatoes and onion and continue to cook for 3 minutes. Add the beef stock, cherry tomatoes and Worcestershire sauce and season with salt and black pepper, according to taste. Cook for a further 2-3 minutes.

4. Adjust seasoning, if required and sprinkle over with chopped chives. Serve hot with warm, crusty bread and a choice of vegetables.

Karahi-Cooked Chicken & Chapattis (Serves 4-6)

Ingredients
450g/1 lb chicken breast (diced)
115ml/1/2 cup of chicken stock
1-2 cloves of garlic (crushed)
2 tbsps vegetable oil
1 small onion (finely chopped)
1 bay leaf
1 tbsp fresh coriander leaves (chopped)
2 tbsps garam masala
1 tsp ground coriander seeds
1/2 tsp dried mint
salt (to season)

Method
1. Heat the vegetable oil in a preheated karahi, (you can use a large wok if you don't own a karahi). Add the onion and garlic and stir-fry for 3-4 minutes, until the onions are tender and golden.

2. Add the ground coriander, bay leaf, garam masala and mint and mix in. Add the chicken and cook, stirring frequently, for 5-6 minutes – sealing the chicken.

3. Pour in the chicken stock and bring just to the boil. Reduce the heat and simmer for 10-12 minutes, until the sauce has thickened.

4. Remove from the heat and stir in the chopped coriander. Season with salt. Serve immediately, with warmed chapattis and a side salad.

Quick Pasta Sauce (Serves 4)

Ingredients
500-600g/5-6 cups of dried spaghetti
1 large tomato (chopped into small pieces)
1 clove of garlic
1/2 tsp dried basil
1/2 tsp dried oregano
1 tbsp olive oil
Parmesan cheese (grated)

Method
1. Place the tomato pieces in a bowl and sprinkle with oregano and basil. Add the olive oil and mix together.

2. Place the garlic clove, whole, in a saucepan and add enough water to boil the pasta in. Bring to the boil and add the pasta, cook as per packet instructions.

3. Drain the pasta thoroughly and return to the saucepan. Add the tomato mixture and toss together. Serve immediately, with a sprinkling of Parmesan cheese, if desired.

Sardine & Tomato Bruschetta (Serves 4)

Ingredients
4 large farmhouse bread rolls (cut in half)
500g/1.1 lbs tinned sardines (in tomato sauce)
785g/3 1/2 cups of canned, chopped tomatoes (drained)
1-2 red onions (finely chopped)
1-2 cloves of garlic (crushed)
2 tbsps olive oil
handful of fresh basil (chopped)
salt & black pepper (to season)

Method

1. Preheat the oven to 220C/425F/Gas mark 7. Place the garlic, onion, basil, tomatoes and olive oil in a bowl and mix together. Season with salt and black pepper, according to taste.

2. Place the rolls in the oven for 2 minutes, then remove and top each half with the tomato mixture. Add the sardines and return the oven for 3-4 minutes. Serve immediately.

Welsh Rabbit (Serves 4)

Ingredients
8 slices of bread
500g/5 cups of cheddar cheese (grated)
4 tsps butter
3 tsps wholegrain mustard
6-8 tbsps beer/ale
2-3 tsps Worcestershire sauce

Method

1. Place the butter, ale, mustard, cheese and Worcestershire sauce in a saucepan and place over a low/medium heat, until melted into a paste-like consistency. Leave to cool.

2. Toast the bread under a grill on both sides, until golden. Remove from the grill and spread the cooled cheese paste over one side of the toast. Return to the grill and cook until the cheese paste turns golden brown

Dinners

Cheese, Bacon & Cauliflower Gratin (Serves 4-6)

Ingredients

1 head of cauliflower (cut into florets)
100g/1 cup of cheddar cheese (grated)
25g/1/4 cup of parmesan cheese (grated)
395ml/1 3/4 cups of chicken or vegetable stock
1/4 cup of spring onions (sliced)
2 eggs
55g/1/4 cup of cream cheese
2 tbsps sour cream
2 tbsps butter
110g/1/2 cup of cooked, chopped bacon pieces
1/2 tsp paprika (more if desired)
salt & black pepper (to season)

Method

1. Place the cauliflower and stock in a saucepan and bring to the boil. Reduce the heat, cover and simmer for 10-12 minutes, until tender.

2. Drain the cauliflower and return to the saucepan over a gentle heat; cook for 1-2 minutes.

3. Transfer the cauliflower into a food processor, followed by the cream cheese, sour cream, butter, spring onions, eggs and half of the cheddar cheese. Season with salt and black pepper and pulse to combine the ingredients – do not puree.

4. Transfer the combined mixture into a large bowl and fold in the chopped bacon pieces.

5. Lightly grease a casserole dish and pour the mixture in. Spread evenly and sprinkle over the top with the remaining cheddar cheese and the parmesan cheese.

6. Sprinkle the paprika over the top of the mixture and place in the oven for 40-45 minutes, until golden brown.

Chicken & Mushroom Casserole (Serves 4-6)

Ingredients

6 chicken breasts (skinless & diced)
1 225g/8oz can of cream of chicken soup
225g/2 1/4 cups of mushrooms (sliced)
110g/1/2 cup of diced bacon
225g/1 cup of long grain wild rice
225ml/1 cup of water
1 tbsp vegetable oil
1 tsp butter
1 tsp mixed herbs
salt & black pepper (to season)

Method

1. This dish is to be cooked in a slow cooker at a low temperature. Heat the butter and oil in a frying pan and add the chicken and mushrooms. Sauté until the chicken is lightly browned.

2. Place the bacon in the bottom of the slow cooker, followed by the rice. Add the chicken and mushrooms and pour in the soup and water.

3. Sprinkle over the mixed herbs and season with salt and black pepper, according to taste. Cover and cook for 5 to 6 hours, until the rice is cooked.

Chilli Con Carne (Serves 4)

Ingredients

500g/1.1lbs of beef mince
800g/2 lbs red kidney beans (drained & rinsed)
2 onions (finely chopped)
2 garlic cloves (crushed)
300ml/1 1/3 cups of beef stock
75g/1/3 cup of tomato puree
55g/1/4 cup of butter
2 tsps chilli powder
3 tsps cumin powder
black pepper (to season)

Method

1. Melt the butter in a large saucepan and add the garlic and onions. Cook for 4-5 minutes until golden brown. Add the beef and cook for 8-10 minutes, browning the beef.

2. Place the cumin, chilli powder and tomato puree in a small bowl and mix together well. Stir into the beef and continue to cook.

3. Add the beef stock, kidney beans and season with black pepper, according to taste. Bring to the boil. Reduce the heat, cover and simmer for 25-30 minutes. Serve piping hot with boiled rice, crusty bread or as a jacket potato topping!

Lamb Meatloaf (Serves 4)

Ingredients

265g/1 3/4 cups of cooked, minced lamb
1 1/2 aubergines (chopped)
1 onion (finely chopped)
1 egg
1 tbsp tomato puree
8 tbsps olive oil
2 tbsps fresh coriander (chopped)
1/2 tsp chilli powder
1/2 tsp ground ginger
1/2 tsp cumin seeds
2 cloves of garlic (crushed)
1 tbsp salt
1 tsp butter
salt & black pepper (to season)

Method

1. Place the minced lamb in a bowl and add the onion, coriander, garlic, tomato puree and spices. Season with salt and black pepper and mix together well. Place in the refrigerator and leave for at least 45 minutes.

2. Cut the aubergine into thin slices, crossways and place on a plate. Sprinkle over the top with salt and leave for 25-30 minutes. Preheat the oven to 180C/350F/Gas mark 4. Grease a loaf tin with butter.

3. Wash the aubergine slices under cold, running water and pat dry with paper kitchen towel. Heat the oil in a large frying pan and add the aubergine slices. Cook for about 10 minutes, turning once. Remove from the heat with a slotted spoon and drain on paper kitchen towel. Leave to one side.

4. Stir the egg into the lamb mixture, binding it well. Layer half of the lamb mixture along the base of the loaf tin, pressing down firmly. Layer with the aubergine slices and top with the remaining lamb mixture.

5 Place in the oven and bake for 35-40 minutes. Remove from the oven and cut into slices to serve. Season with salt & pepper.

Lamb Stroganoff (Serves 4)

Ingredients

525g/3 1/2 cups of cooked lamb (cubed)
450ml/2 cups of lamb stock
250ml/1 cup of cream or crème fraiche
20-25 chestnut mushrooms (sliced)
2 medium onions (sliced)
1-2 cloves of garlic (crushed)
4 tbsps plain flour
1/2 tsp paprika
1 tsp dried rosemary
50g/1/4 cup of butter
2 tbsps dry white wine
Salt & black pepper (to season)

Method

1. Heat the butter in a frying pan and add the garlic and onions. Cook for 3-4 minutes, until tender. Add the lamb and cook for 2-3 minutes, heating it through.

2. Add the mushrooms and cook for a further 2 minutes. Remove the contents of the frying pan with a slotted spoon and keep them warm.

3. Place the flour, paprika and dried rosemary in a bowl and mix together well. Sprinkle the flour mixture over the fat in the pan and stir well. Cook for 1-2 minutes and add the dry white wine, followed by the stock. Cook, stirring continuously, for 1 minute.

4. Remove from the heat and gradually add the cream/crème fraiche, stirring continuously. Return to the heat and stir until smooth, (add a little milk if the sauce is too thick).

5. Stir in the lamb mixture and heat through for 3-4 minutes. Season with salt and pepper and serve immediately over a bed of rice.

Dinners

Macaroni Cheese Bake (Serves 4)

Ingredients

210g/4/5 cup of canned creamed mushrooms
250g/2 1/4 cups of cooked macaroni
225g/1 1/2 cups of ham (finely chopped)
395g/1 3/4 cups of canned chopped tomatoes
110g/1/2 cup of tomato puree
1 onion (finely chopped)
2 cloves of garlic (crushed)
4 tbsps dry white wine
50g/1/2 cup of parmesan cheese (grated)
3 tbsps butter
1 tsp sugar
1 tbsp fresh parsley (finely chopped)
salt & black pepper (to season)

Method

1. Heat the butter in a frying pan and add the garlic and onion. Cook for 3-4 minutes, until tender. Remove with a slotted spoon.

2. Place the macaroni in a large bowl and add the onion, garlic, ham, creamed mushrooms, white wine, tomatoes, sugar and tomato puree in a bowl and combine well. Season with salt and black pepper, according to taste.

3. Transfer to an ovenproof casserole dish, cover and place in the oven for 40-45 minutes, until piping hot.

4. Remove from the oven and sprinkle with parmesan cheese and chopped parsley. Serve immediately.

Mixed Vegetable Curry (Serves 4-6)

Ingredients

260g/1 1/2 cups of potatoes (diced)
130g/3/4 cup of sweet potatoes (diced)
160g/1/2 cup of cauliflower florets
1 small courgette (diced)
4-5 carrots (diced)
180g/1 cup of green beans (sliced)
1 onion (sliced)
4 tomatoes (skinless & chopped)
1 tsp turmeric
2 tsps ground coriander
1 tsp ground cumin
1 tsp chilli powder
375ml/1 2/3 cups of hot vegetable stock
3 tbsps vegetable oil

Method

1. Heat the vegetable oil in a large saucepan and add the onion. Cook for 4-5 minutes, until tender.

2. Add the chilli powder, coriander, cumin and turmeric, cooking for 2-3 minutes and stirring frequently.

3. Add the cauliflower florets, courgettes, sweet potatoes, potatoes, carrots and green beans; coating them well with the spices.

4. Add the chopped tomatoes and vegetable stock and bring to the boil. Reduce the heat and simmer for 10-13 minutes, until the vegetables are tender.

5. Serve immediately with hot rice.

Pork Chops with Sweet Potato Mash (Serves 6)

Ingredients
5 pork chops (with bone)
750g/4 1/4 sweet potatoes (peeled & sliced)
500ml/2 1/4 cups of medium-sweet cider
3 tbsps crème fraiche
1 1/2 tbsps Dijon mustard
30g/1/8 cup of butter
25g/1 cup of fresh flat-leaf parsley (finely chopped)
black pepper (to season)

Method
1. Preheat the grill to a medium heat. Cook the pork chops for 20 minutes, turning every 5 minutes. Whilst the chops are cooking, boil the sweet potatoes for 13-15 minutes, until tender.

2. Whilst the potatoes are cooking, place the cider and Dijon mustard in a saucepan and bring to the boil. Simmer until the liquid has reduced by half.

3. Drain the cooked potatoes and mash together, adding the butter and black pepper. Cover and set aside, keeping the mash warm.

4. Once the cider/mustard liquid has reduced sufficiently, stir in the crème fraiche. Equally serve out the sweet potato mash on individual plates and top each with a pork chop. Spoon the sauce over the top and sprinkle with a little chopped parsley.

Potato & Cheese Bake (Serves 4-6)

Ingredients for bake
1kg/2.2 lbs waxy potatoes (peeled & cut into 1/4 inch slices)
100g/1 cup of cheddar cheese (grated)

Ingredients for sauce
845g/3 3/4 cups of canned, chopped tomatoes (with juices)
2 tbsps tomato puree
250g/2 cups of button mushrooms (sliced)
2 cloves of garlic (crushed)
1 large onion (finely chopped)
1 tbsp olive oil
salt & black pepper (to season)

Method
1. Boil the potato slices for 10-12 minutes, until just tender. Drain and set to one side.

2. To make the sauce, heat the olive oil in a saucepan and add the garlic and onion. Cook over a medium heat for 5-6 minutes, until tender. Stir in the tomato puree, followed by the canned tomatoes. Cook for 1 minute.

3. Add the mushrooms and continue to cook, uncovered, for 12-15 minutes, until the liquid has reduced right down. Season with salt and black pepper, according to taste. Remove from the heat.

4. Preheat the grill to a medium/high heat. Lightly grease a heatproof dish, (one that will fit underneath the grill), and layer half of the potato slices inside the base. Carefully spoon the sauce over the top and sprinkle over with half of the grated cheese.

5. Layer the remaining potatoes over the top and sprinkle over the rest of the cheese. Place under the grill for 5-7 minutes, until heated through and the cheese is golden brown. Serve immediately with a choice of green vegetables.

Dinners

Toad-in-the-Hole (Serves 4)

Ingredients
8 thick pork sausages
145g/1 1/4 cups of plain flour
225ml/1 cup of milk
1 large egg
1 onion (chopped)
3 tbsps vegetable oil
2 tbsps fresh thyme (chopped)
5 tbsps water
black pepper (to season)

Method
1. Preheat the oven to 200C/400F/Gas mark 6. Heat one tablespoon of vegetable oil in a frying pan and add the sausages. Cook over a medium heat for 6-8 minutes, until browned.

2. Place the flour and egg in a bowl and gradually whisk in the water and milk. Add the chopped thyme and season with black pepper, according to taste.

3. Place the remaining vegetable oil in an ovenproof casserole dish. Place the dish in the oven for a couple of minutes to heat the oil.

4. Remove the dish from the oven and add the browned sausages and chopped onion. Pour the batter evenly over the top of the sausages and place in the oven. Cook for 35-40 minutes, until golden brown and risen.

Dinners

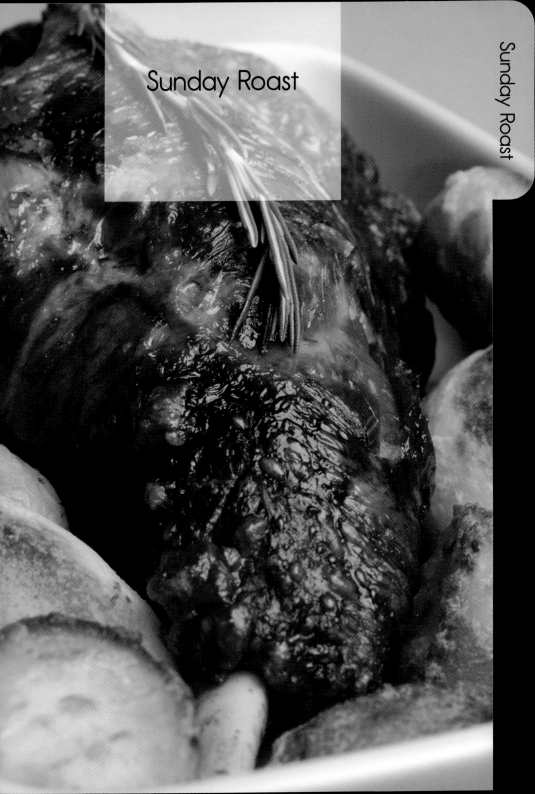

Sunday Roast

Aromatic Chicken Roast (Serves 4)

Ingredients
1.3 to 1.5kg/3 lbs chicken
1 lemon (halved)
2 onions (chopped)
olive oil
salt & black pepper (to season)

Method
1. Preheat the oven to 180C/350F/Gas mark 4. Insert the lemon halves inside the chicken. Distribute the chopped onion over the base of a roasting pan, (one that will allow the chicken to fit in quite snugly), and place the chicken on top.

2. Pour some olive oil onto the chicken and smear all over. Season with salt and black pepper and rub in well, using your hands.

3. Turn the chicken on its side and place in the oven for 30 minutes. Turn again to the other side and cook for a further 30 minutes. Turn the chicken for the last time, breast-side up and cook for a further 30 minutes – or for the remaining cooking time, dependant on the weight of the chicken.

4. Remove from the oven and test that the chicken is cooked by piercing the thickest part of the leg with a skewer – the juices should run clear.

5. Transfer to a serving dish and stand in a warm place for 15 minutes before carving.

Bread Sauce (Serves 4)

Ingredients
280ml/1 1/4 cups of milk
100g day-old, white bread (crusts removed & torn into small pieces)
1/2 onion (finely chopped)
1/4 tsp ground cloves
30g/1/8 cup of butter
2 tbsps double cream
1 fresh bay leaf (torn in half)
1/4 tsp freshly grated nutmeg
knob of butter
black pepper (to season)

Method
1. Place the milk, butter, onion, ground cloves and bay leaf in a saucepan and season with black pepper.

2. Bring to the boil. Reduce the heat and simmer for 20 minutes. Remove from the heat, cover and leave for at least 1 hour for the flavours to infuse. If you have time, refrigerate over night to bring out maximum flavour.

3. Remove the bay leaf and stir the bread into the milk mixture, using a wooden spoon. Add the nutmeg and season, according to taste.

4. Return the saucepan to the heat and bring to the boil. Reduce the heat and simmer for 4-5 minutes. Stir in the cream and remove from the heat.

5. Serve warm.

Chilli Roast Potatoes (Serves 4-6)

Ingredients
1kg/2.2 lbs potatoes (peeled & cut into 2 inch chunks)
1/2 tsp chilli powder
2 tsps paprika powder
6 tbsps olive oil
1 1/2 tbsps sesame oil
1 tbsp fresh coriander (chopped)
salt & black pepper (to season)

Method
1. Preheat the oven to 200C/400F/Gas mark 6. Boil the potatoes for 5 minutes.

2. Drain thoroughly, return to the saucepan and remove any excess water by shaking the pan over a low heat.

3. Place a lid over the saucepan and shake the potatoes well, to roughen the edges.

4. Heat the oil in a roasting tin and stir in the paprika and chilli powders. Add the potatoes and season with salt and black pepper, according to taste.

5. Place in the oven for 45-50 minutes, basting frequently with the hot oil.

6. Remove from the oven and transfer to a serving dish. Garnish with coriander and serve immediately.

Colcannon Mash (Serves 4-6)
Ingredients
875g/5 cups of potatoes (peeled & cut into chunks)
1/2 savoy cabbage (finely shredded)
bunch of spring onions (finely chopped)
1-2 tsp butter
1-2 tbsps milk

Method
1. Preheat the oven to 200C/400F/Gas mark 6. Boil the potatoes for 12-15 minutes, until soft. For the last 7-9 minutes, add the shredded cabbage.

2. Drain thoroughly and add the butter and milk. Mash well and stir through the chopped spring onions, setting aside a few for garnishing.

3. Serve hot.

Cranberry Sauce with Port (Serves 4)

Ingredients
200g/2 cups of fresh cranberries
2 tbsps orange flower honey
30ml/1/8 cup of port
juice of 2 Clementines
1 Clementine (peeled & in segments)
40g/1/3 cup of light muscovado sugar
1 star anise

Method
1. Place the sugar, cranberries, honey and Clementine juice in a saucepan and heat. Cook, bubbling gently, for 10 minutes until the cranberries are tender.

2. Taste and add a little more sugar if needed. Add the port and star anise. Bring to a gentle boil and cook for 2 minutes. Remove from the heat.

3. Leave to cool a little for a few minutes and then add the Clementine segments, stirring them gently into the sauce. Best served with poultry.

Honey-Roast Gammon (Serves 4-6)

Ingredients
1.6 to 1.8kg/3.5 - 4lbs gammon joint
(soaked in cold water for 3-4 hours)
2 tbsps runny honey
2 tbsps wholegrain mustard
juice & rind of 1 orange
1 onion
2 tbsps soft brown sugar
10 peppercorns
18 whole cloves
2 bay leaves

Method
. Drain the gammon and place in a large saucepan. Stud the onion with
3 of the cloves and add to the saucepan, followed by the peppercorns and
bay leaves.

2. Cover the joint with cold water and bring to the boil. Reduce the heat,
cover and simmer for 1 hour.

3. Preheat the oven to 200C/400F/Gas mark 6. Drain the gammon and set
aside for 5 minutes.

4. Remove the skin and the majority of its fat, leaving a little. Mark the
remaining fat into scored diamonds and stud with the remaining cloves.
Place the joint into a roasting tin.

5. Place the honey, mustard, brown sugar and the juice and rind of the
orange in a bowl; mix together well. Pour the glaze evenly over the
gammon joint.

6. Place in the oven and roast for 40-45 minutes, basting the joint well every
10-15 minutes. Remove from the oven and leave to stand for 10-15 minutes
before slicing.

Leg of Lamb with Roasted Vegetables (Serves 4)
Ingredients
1.8kg/4 lbs whole leg of lamb
4 shallots (whole)
4 carrots (whole)
480g/2 3/4 cups of Anya potatoes (or similar)
1 celeriac (peeled & diced)
Juice of 1 orange
a handful of rosemary sprigs

Method
. Preheat the oven to 190C/375F/Gas mark 5. Place the lamb in an
appropriately sized roasting tin and lay the rosemary on top.

Leg of Lamb with Roasted Vegetables/cont.

2. Place the lamb in the oven and roast for 1 hour and 20 minutes. Remove the lamb from the oven and add the carrots, shallots, potatoes and celeriac.

3. Pour the orange juice over the vegetables and place back in the oven. Roast for 30 minutes, turning the vegetables halfway.

4. Remove from the oven and leave the lamb to rest for 10 minutes before serving, (whilst keeping the vegetables warm).

Mixed Roasted Vegetables & Potatoes (Serves 4-6)

Ingredients
1.25kg/2 3/4 lbs mixed root vegetables, such as; sweet potatoes, carrots, swede, parsnips, potatoes (peeled & cut into large chunks)
225g/1/2 lb whole shallots (peeled)
3 sprigs of fresh thyme
3 sprigs of fresh rosemary
2 tbsps olive oil
1 tsp rock salt
1 tsp fresh black peppercorns

Method
1. Preheat the oven to 220C/425F/Gas mark 7. Place all the vegetables in a saucepan and cover with boiling water. Bring to the boil, reduce the heat and simmer for 6-7 minutes.

2. Drain the vegetables and shallots and place in an appropriately sized roasting tin. Brush the vegetables with the oil and sprinkle over with salt and black peppercorns.

3. Evenly place the herb sprigs in the roasting tin and place in the centre of the oven. Roast for 35-40 minutes, turning halfway through cooking. Remove from the oven when golden brown and crisp. Serve immediately.

Pork Roast with Roasted Vegetables (Serves 4)

Ingredients

750g/1 2/3 lbs pork rib roast (trimmed)
red cabbage (shredded)
8 carrots (peeled & cut into 2 inch pieces)
shallots (whole)
480g/2 3/4 cups of Anya potatoes (or similar)
clove of garlic (crushed)
tbsp brown sugar
tbsp red wine vinegar
1/4 tsp ground cinnamon
1/4 tsp freshly ground nutmeg
1/4 tsp ground cloves
4 tbsps olive oil
black pepper (to season)

Method

1. Preheat the oven to 190C/375F/Gas mark 5. Place the pork rib in an appropriately sized roasting tin and cover with foil. Place in the oven for 1 hour and 15 minutes, removing the foil for the last 20 minutes of cooking.

2. Whilst the pork is cooking, boil the carrots, potatoes and shallots for 5 minutes, (in separate pans). Drain and rinse under cold water.

3. Transfer the carrots, potatoes and shallots to a roasting tin and drizzle over two tablespoons of olive oil. Gently toss the vegetables in the olive oil and season with black pepper. Place in the oven for the last 40-45 minutes of the pork rib cooking time.

4. Once the pork rib is cooked remove from the oven and set aside to rest for 10-15 minutes before carving.

5. Heat the remaining olive oil in a saucepan and add the garlic. Cook over a medium heat for 2-3 minutes. Add the shredded red cabbage and cook for 4-5 minutes.

6. Add the ground nutmeg, cloves and cinnamon and stir into the cabbage. Cover and cook for a further 4-5 minutes. Remove from the heat and stir in the vinegar and sugar. Serve the pork with the roasted vegetables and red cabbage.

Potato & Carrot Mash (Serves 4)

Ingredients
1kg/2.2 lbs potatoes (peeled & cut into chunks)
450g/3 cups of carrots (peeled & sliced)
60ml/1/4 cup of double cream
75ml/1/3 cup dry white wine
black pepper (to season)

Method
1. Boil the potatoes for 12-13 minutes, until just tender. Add the carrots and cook for a further 5-6 minutes. Drain thoroughly.

2. Mash the carrots and potatoes well and season with black pepper. Pour the white wine and double cream in a saucepan and heat to just boiling.

3. Reduce the heat and simmer gently for 2 minutes. Do not burn. Pour the mixture into the mash, stirring it until fluffy. Serve immediately.

Roast Turkey with Orange Glaze (Serves 4)

Ingredients
2.5kg turkey (giblets removed)
juice & rind of 1 orange
30g/1/8 cup of caster sugar
1/2 tsp fresh rosemary (chopped)
1/2 tsp white wine vinegar
2 tbsps olive oil
Fresh cranberries (to garnish)
1 tbsp butter

Method
1. Preheat the oven to 190C/375F/Gas mark 5. Place the turkey in an appropriately sized roasting tin and brush with olive oil. Cover with foil, lightly greased with butter.

2. Place in the oven for 1 hour and 25 minutes, (or as per pack instructions – until the juices run clear).

3. Baste every 20 minutes to keep the turkey moist. Remove the foil 20 minutes before the end of cooking time.

4. Whilst the turkey is cooking, place the orange juice and rind, white wine vinegar and sugar in a saucepan. Bring to the boil and then reduce the heat. Simmer until the orange juice has reduced to a thick glaze.

5. Add the rosemary to the orange glaze, stirring it in well. Pour evenly over the turkey 20 minutes before the end of cooking time.

6. Remove the turkey from the oven and leave for 15-20 minutes before carving. Garnish with cranberries and serve with seasonal vegetables.

Spiced Roast Beef (Serves 4)

Ingredients
500g/1.1 lbs prime beef rib roasting joint (boneless)
1/2 red chilli (deseeded & chopped)
1/2 tsp coriander
1/4 tsp ground cinnamon
1/4 tsp black pepper

Method
1. Preheat the oven to 220C/425F/Gas mark 7. Place the chilli, coriander, cinnamon and black pepper in a small bowl and mix together.

2. Place the beef in an appropriately sized roasting tin and rub the spice mixture into the meat. Roast in the oven for 15 minutes and then remove. Baste the meat with the juices.

3. Reduce the oven to 180C/350F/Gas mark 4. Return the beef to the oven and roast for a further 20-25 minutes, or until cooked to your preference. Baste halfway through the remaining cooking time.

4. Remove from the oven and set aside to stand for 15-20 minutes before carving.

Puddings

Puddings

Banana Splits (Serves 6)

Ingredients

450g/1 lb vanilla ice cream
225ml/1 cup of double cream
6 large bananas
6 glace cherries
35-40g walnuts (chopped)

Method

1. Whip the double cream in a bowl, until slightly stiff. Peel and split the bananas lengthways and fill with equal amounts of ice cream. Sandwich the two halves together of each banana and place on individual serving plates.

2. Top the bananas with the whipped cream and sprinkle with chopped walnuts. Pop a cherry on top of each! Serve immediately with chocolate dessert sauce (optional).

Bread & Butter Pudding (Serves 4-6)

Ingredients

115g/3/4 cup of sultanas
3 tbsps orange marmalade (thick-cut)
7-8 slices white bread (crusts removed)
55g/1/4 cup of butter (softened)
225ml/1 cup of double cream
225ml/1 cup of milk
3 eggs
55g/1/4 cup of caster sugar
1/2 tsp vanilla essence
icing sugar (for dusting)

Method

1. Preheat the oven to 190C/375F/Gas mark 5. Lightly butter a shallow ovenproof dish.

2. Spread butter on one side of each slice of bread, then spread with marmalade. Arrange some of the bread, marmalade side-up, covering the base of the ovenproof dish. Cut any remaining bread into triangles.

3. Sprinkle over the top of the bread with sultanas and then arrange the bread triangles over the top.

4. Place the milk, eggs, caster sugar and double cream in a bowl and whisk together well. Stir in the vanilla essence.

5. Push through a sieve into a pouring jug and pour over the bread mixture in the dish. Leave to soak for 3-5 minutes.

6. Place the dish inside a large roasting tin and half fill it with hot water.

7. Place in the oven for 25-30 minutes, until the top is golden brown and the custard is setting, but not firm. Remove from the oven and leave to cool for 10 minutes. Dust with icing sugar.

8. Preheat the grill to a medium setting and place under the grill for 1-2 minutes, until golden. Serve with vanilla ice cream or whipped cream.

Chantilly Meringues (Makes 12)
Ingredients for meringues
260g/1 1/4 cups caster sugar (unrefined)
6 egg whites (beaten)

Ingredients for filling:
600ml/2 1/2 cups double cream
50g/1/4 cup caster sugar (unrefined)
3-4 drops of vanilla extract

Method for meringues
1. Preheat oven to 140C/275F/Gas mark 1. Line 2 baking trays with baking paper.

2. Beat half of the sugar into the beaten eggs; followed by the remaining half – beat well.

3. Spoon the mixture onto the baking trays; 12 spoonfuls per tray. Place in the oven for 2 hours. To ensure that your meringues are crispy, turn the oven off and leave the meringues inside overnight.

Method for filling

1. Place the cream, sugar and vanilla extract in a bowl and whisk together, until soft peaks form. Place a dollop of cream onto 12 of the meringues and then top with the other 12, creating a sandwich.

2. Place in the refrigerator for 1 hour before serving.

Chocolate Mint Ice Cream (Serves 8)

Ingredients

300ml/1 1/3 cups of milk

55g/1/4 cup of caster sugar

5 egg yolks

300g/2/3 lb After Eight mints (or similar soft, dark chocolate mints)

560ml/2 1/2 cups of double cream

Method

1. Break the chocolate mints into small pieces and chill. Place the milk and cream in a saucepan and heat gently, until almost to boiling point. Remove from the heat.

2. Place the sugar and egg yolks in a bowl and beat together, until creamed. Gradually pour the cream/milk mixture over the eggs, whisking continuously.

3. Return the mixture to the pan and heat gently, stirring continuously, until lightly thickened. Strain the mixture through a sieve, into a bowl. Leave to cool completely.

4. Pour into a freezer-safe container and freeze for 2-3 hours, until partly frozen. Stir the mixture and return to the freezer. Repeat this process twice more.

5. On the last occasion, stir in the chocolate mints, folding them in evenly. Return to the freezer for 7-8 hours, until firm. Remove from the freezer for 20-30 minutes to soften a little prior to serving.

Chocolate Mousse (Makes 12)

Ingredients
225g/1/2 lb dark chocolate (broken into pieces)
310ml/1 1/4 cups of double cream
3 eggs (separated)
3 tbsps caster sugar
24 chocolate dessert decorations

Method
1. Firstly, melt the chocolate in a glass bowl either in the microwave, (on defrost setting) or over a saucepan of boiling water. Leave to cool on one side for 3-5 minutes.

2. Place the cream in a bowl and beat with an electric hand mixer, until soft peaks form.

3. Beat the egg whites in a separate bowl, until soft peaks form. Add the sugar and beat for 2 minutes, until the sugar has dissolved and the mixture has thickened.

4. Stir the egg yolks into the saucepan of cooled chocolate with a metal spoon – stir until well combined. Stir 1/3 of the egg/sugar mixture into the chocolate mixture, mixing together well. Repeat twice more until combined.

5. Carefully fold in the whipped cream. Transfer the mixture into a large icing bag. Equally pipe the mixture into the dessert glasses and cover with cling wrap.

6. Chill in the refrigerator for 4-5 hours, until set. Decorate with chocolate dessert shapes and serve.

Chocolate Raisin Cookies (Makes 36)

Ingredients

50g/1/2 cup of wholewheat flour
30g/1/4 cup of plain flour
100g/3 1/2oz chocolate raisins
/4 tsp baking powder
/2 tbsp molasses
110g/1/2 cup of butter (softened)
110g/1/2 cup of light brown sugar
1 egg (lightly beaten)
150g/1 1/2 cups of rolled oats (not instant)
/2 tsp ground cinnamon
/4 tsp ground nutmeg
pinch of allspice

Method

1. Place the plain flour, wholewheat flour, cinnamon, allspice, nutmeg and baking powder in a bowl and mix together.

2. Place the molasses, butter and brown sugar in a large bowl and beat with a hand-held electric blender. Beat for a few minutes, until the mixture becomes light and fluffy. Beat in the egg. Gradually add the flour and spice mixture, mixing in a little at a time.

3. Carefully fold in the chocolate raisins and rolled oats; combine well with a wooden spoon. Place the dough in the refrigerator for 45-60 minutes, until the dough is fairly firm.

4. Whilst the dough is firming, preheat the oven to 180C/350F/Gas mark 4 and line 4 baking trays with baking paper.

5. Remove the dough from the fridge and scoop out the dough, one per tablespoon. Roll each dough piece into a ball and gently flatten.

6. Place the cookies onto the baking trays, 1 1/2 inches apart. Place in the oven for 16-18 minutes, until golden brown. Remove from the oven and leave to cool for 6-8 minutes. Transfer the cookies to a wire cooling rack to cool completely.

Chocolate Slices (Serves 10-12)

Ingredients
16 digestive biscuits (crushed)
55g/1/4 cup of glace cherries (chopped)
50g/2/3 cup of slivered flaked almonds
100g/3/4 cup of dark chocolate (melted)
55g/1/4 cup of butter (melted)
1 tbsp orange juice
2 tsps ground allspice

Method
1. Place the biscuits, almonds, allspice and cherries in a bowl and mix together well. Add the orange juice, melted butter and chocolate.

2. Transfer the mixture to a shallow cake tin and spread evenly, smoothing the surface with the back of a spoon.

3. Refrigerate for 2-3 hours, (or longer if preferred), until set. Cut into slices and serve.

Frozen Yoghurt with Cherry Sauce (Serves 4)

Ingredients
75ml/1/3 cup of double cream
180ml/3/4 cup of natural yoghurt
1 egg white
170g/3/4 cup of cherries (pitted)
60g/1/2 cup of caster sugar
75ml/1/3 cup of water
1 tsp arrowroot
1 tbsp icing sugar
grated dark chocolate (to serve)

Method
1. Place the water, caster sugar and cherries in a pan and bring to the boil. Reduce the heat and simmer for 4 minutes.

2. Remove from the heat, strain the juices and reserve. Remove 3-4 cherries, slice and place to one side.

3. Place the remaining cherries in a food processor and blend until pureed. Press the cherries through a sieve into a bowl and leave to one side for 2-3 minutes.

4. Place the cream in a bowl and lightly whip. Stir into the cherry puree, followed by the yoghurt. Mix well.

5. Place the egg white in a bowl and whisk until stiffened. Add the icing sugar and whisk again, until peaks form. Carefully fold into the cherry - yoghurt mixture. Transfer to a freezer-safe container and freeze for 3-4 hours, until firm.

6. Place the arrowroot in a bowl and add a little water to make a paste. Stir into the reserved cherry juice and add the cherry slices. Transfer to a saucepan and bring to the boil, reduce the heat and simmer for 3-4 minutes, until thickened.

7. Remove from the heat and leave to cool. Once cooled, cover and refrigerate. Remove the frozen cherry yoghurt from the freezer and place in the refrigerator for 1 1/2 -2 hours, to soften.

8. Spoon the yoghurt into serving bowls and top with the cherry sauce. Sprinkle over with dark chocolate and serve immediately.

Fruity Chocolate Refrigerator Cake (Serves 8-12)

Ingredients

225g/2 1/4 cups of ginger nut biscuits, broken
175g/6oz dark chocolate, chopped into small pieces
25g/1oz sultanas
25g/1oz glace cherries, chopped
25g/1oz dried cherries
25g/1oz mixed peel
25g/1oz flaked almonds
150g/2/3 cup of unsalted butter
4 tbsps double cream

Method

1. Line a cake tin with foil and brush the foil lightly with oil. Place the ginger nut biscuits, fruit, peel and almonds in a bowl and combine well.

2. Place the butter, cream and chocolate in a pan and place over a low heat, stir until the chocolate is melted and the mixture is smooth.

3. Pour the melted chocolate mix over the biscuit/fruit mix in the bowl and stir together.

4. Spoon the mixture into the cake tin and press down firmly and evenly. Cover the cake mix with foil and refrigerate for 2 1/2-3 hours.

5. Remove from the refrigerator and turn out onto a plate, peeling off the foil. To serve, cut into slices. Serve with vanilla or chocolate ice cream!

Knickerbocker Glory! (Makes 6)

Ingredients
250ml/1 cup of double cream
375g/3 cups vanilla ice cream
375g/3 cups chocolate ice cream
75g/2 1/2oz chocolate (broken into pieces)
340g/1 1/2 cups of strawberries (hulled & halved)
6 peaches (peeled & cut into thin slices)
4-6 large cherries (pitted)
5 tbsps brandy (optional)
43g/1/4 cup of chocolate chips (optional)

Method

1. Divide the strawberries equally and place at the base of 6 tall sundae glasses.

2. Place a scoop of vanilla ice cream in each glass and top with equal amounts of peach slices. Top with a scoop of chocolate ice cream.

3. Place the chocolate and brandy in a bowl and gently heat, stirring continuously. Melt and combine the chocolate with the brandy and then pour a little over the top of the chocolate ice cream.

4. Place the double cream in a bowl and beat until stiff peaks form. Spoon on top of the sundaes and decorate with cherries. Add a few chocolate chips, if you're feeling a bit naughty!

Raspberry Fool (Serves 4)

Ingredients
150ml/2/3 cup of double cream
170ml/2/3 cup of natural yoghurt
250g/2 cups of raspberries
50g/1/2 cup of caster sugar
4 fresh mint leaves

Method
1. Place the raspberries in a glass bowl and crush them with a fork. Add the sugar and mix together well. Leave to one side for 15 minutes.

2. Place the cream in a bowl and beat until thickened. Gradually add the yoghurt, bit by bit, beating it thoroughly.

3. Swirl the raspberry mixture into the yoghurt/cream mixture. Do not combine completely, as this will mix the colours too much.

4. Spoon into glass dessert bowls and garnish with mint. Place in the refrigerator for 2-3 hours before serving.

Vanilla Cheesecake (Serves 4-6)

Ingredients for base
175g/1 3/4 cups of digestive biscuits (crushed)
75g/1/3 cup of butter (melted)
1 tbsp sugar

Ingredients for topping
1kg/8 1/2 cups of cream cheese
150ml/2/3 cup of sour cream
3 eggs
1 egg yolk
180g/1 1/4 cups of caster sugar
3 tbsps flour

1 vanilla pod (scraped)
2 tsps lemon juice
zest of 1 lemon

Method for base
1. Preheat the oven to 180C/350F/Gas mark 4. Line a 24cm spring-base cake tin. Place the crushed biscuits, sugar and melted butter in a bowl and mix together well. Press into the cake tin.

2. Place in the oven for 10 minutes. Remove from the oven and increase the oven heat to 200C/400F/Gas mark 6.

Method for topping
1. Place the cream cheese in a bowl and soften with a wooden spoon. Add the flour and sugar and whisk together.

2. Stir in the vanilla, lemon juice and lemon zest, followed by the 3 eggs and 1 egg yolk; adding the eggs one at a time and whisking them in after each new addition.

3. Add the sour cream and whisk in. Pour over the biscuit base and place in the oven for 8-10 minutes.

4. Reduce the oven to 110C/225F/Gas mark 4 and bake for 30-35 minutes, until set.

5. Remove from the oven and leave to cool. Chill in the refrigerator for 2-3 hours before serving.

Celebrations

Celebrations

Celebration Cupcakes (Makes 24)

Ingredients for cupcakes
260g/2 1/4 cups of self-raising flour
225g/1 cup of margarine (softened)
225g/1 cup of caster sugar
4 eggs
2 tsps vanilla essence

Ingredients for icing
225g/1 cup of icing sugar
1/2 tsp chosen food colouring
lemon juice
3 1/2 tbsps water
Decorations, such as marshmallows, sweets, chocolate chips, silver balls, etc

Method for cupcakes
1. Heat the oven to 180C/350F/Gas mark 4. Line 2 muffin/cupcake tins with paper cases.

2. Place all of the ingredients in a bowl and beat together well, until smooth and creamy in colour.

3. Spoon the mixture into the cupcake paper liners, up to about 2/3 full. Place in the oven for 18-20 minutes, until the cakes have risen and are golden in colour.

4. Leave to cool a little for 2-3 minutes and then transfer to a wire cooling rack. Leave to cool completely.

Method for icing
1. Place the water, lemon juice, icing sugar and food colouring in a bowl and mix well. Spread smoothly onto each individual cooled cupcake.

2. Decorate the top with your choice of decorations – for kids' parties, make funny faces and animals, they'll love it!

Cheese Sticks (Serves 8)

Ingredients
100g/1 cup of cheddar cheese (grated)
110g/1/2 cup of butter (cut into small pieces)
2 eggs (beaten)
50g/1/2 cup of Parmesan cheese (grated)
200g/1 3/4 cups of plain flour
salt & black pepper (to season)

Method
1. Preheat the oven to 200C/400F/Gas mark 6. Sift the salt and flour in a bowl and mix together. Rub in the butter with your hands to make breadcrumbs.

2. Stir in the cheese and add 3/4 of the beaten eggs. Bind together and knead into a dough.

3. Sprinkle some flour over a clean work surface and roll out the dough. Brush over the top with the remaining egg and sprinkle over the top with Parmesan cheese.

4. Cut into 6cm x 0.5cm sticks and place on the baking sheets. Place in the oven for 8-10 minutes, until golden. Remove from the oven and transfer to a wire rack to cool.

Chicken & Bacon Skewers (Serves 12)

Ingredients

12 chicken breasts (skinless)
12 slices of smoked back bacon
 cloves of garlic (crushed)
3 tbsps tomato puree
2 handfuls of fresh basil (finely chopped)
 tbsps olive oil
salt & black pepper (to season)

Method

 Lay a chicken breast between 2 sheets of cling wrap and beat with a rolling pin, until flattened to about 1cm thick. Repeat this process for all the chicken breasts.

2. Place the tomato puree and garlic in a small bowl and mix together. Evenly spread over the chicken breasts, topped by a slice of bacon and a sprinkling of basil. Season with salt and black pepper, according to taste.

3. Roll each chicken breast into a tight roll and then using a sharp knife, cut into 2 inch slices.

4. Keeping the chicken slices rolled up, push them onto metal skewers, (or presoaked wooden skewers), so that they hold a spiral shape.

5. Preheat the grill to a medium/high setting. Brush with olive oil and place under the grill for 10-12 minutes, turning once. Serve hot or cold.

Chocolate-Chip Cupcakes (Makes 12)

Ingredients

175g/1 1/2 cups of self-raising flour
150g/2/3 cup of caster sugar
150g/2/3 cup of butter (softened)
3 eggs (lightly beaten)
50g/1/3 cup of chocolate chips
 tsp vanilla extract

Method
1. Preheat the oven 180C/350F/Gas mark 5. Line a 12-cup cupcake tray with cupcake papers.

2. Place all of the ingredients, (except the chocolate chips), in a large bowl and beat with a handheld electric mixer for 2-3 minutes, until light and creamy.

3. Add the chocolate chips and fold into the mixture. Divide the mixture equally between the cupcake cases.

4. Place in the oven for 18-20 minutes, until firm to the touch and risen. Remove from the oven and leave to cool for a few minutes. Transfer to a wire
cooling rack and leave to cool completely.

Crispy Potato Skins & Tex Mex Dips (Serves 12)

Ingredients
12 large jacket potatoes
150g/1 1/2 cups of cheddar cheese (grated)
olive oil cooking spray (or olive oil)
2 tubs of mild salsa
2 tubs of soured cream with chives
2 tubs of guacamole

Method
1. Preheat the oven to 180C/350F/Gas mark 4. Line 2 baking trays with non-stick baking paper.

2. Place the jacket potatoes in the oven and bake for 1 to 1 1/2 hours, until cooked. Remove from the oven and leave to cool a little for 10-15 minutes.

3. Cut the potatoes in half, lengthways and spoon out the potato inside; leaving about 5mm of potato flesh inside. With a sharp knife, slice each piece into 3 pieces, lengthways.

. Place the potato skins on the baking trays and spray with the cooking oil, or brush with olive oil). Sprinkle over the grated cheese and place in the oven for 20-25 minutes, until gold and crispy. Remove from the oven and leave to cool a little. Serve with the dips!

Fruit Slushies (Makes 10-12)

Ingredients
300g/2 cups of frozen berries (strawberries, raspberries, etc)
300ml/1 1/3 cups of fruit squash (of your preference)
1 litre/4 1/2 cups of cold water
20-25 ice-cubes

Method
1. You will need to do this recipe in batches. Place all of the ingredients into a food processor and blend on the highest speed for 10-12 seconds.

2. Stir the contents and blend for another 8-10 seconds, until smooth, with ice crystals. Spoon into cups and serve with straws or spoons.

Jalapeno Dip

Ingredients
3 tsps jarred, sliced jalapeno peppers & juice
1 tsp paprika
3/4 tsp ground cumin
1/4 tsp cayenne pepper
1 tsp lime juice
1/8 tsp garlic powder
225g/1 cup of mayonnaise
1 tsp sugar
salt (to season)

Method
1. Place all of the ingredients, (except the salt), in a food processor and blend until pureed.

2. Season with salt, according to taste and transfer to a serving bowl. Cover and refrigerate for 20-30 minutes. Serve with tortilla chips or a selection of crudités.

Jalapeno Poppers! (Makes 32)

Ingredients

16 jalapeno peppers (seeded & halved)
225g/2 1/4 cups of cheddar cheese (grated)
350g/3 1/2 cups of cream cheese (softened)
2 tbsps bacon bits
240ml/1 1/8 cup of milk
140g/1 1/4 cups of plain flour
115g/1 1/4 cup of dried breadcrumbs
1.9 litres/8 cups of vegetable oil

Method

1. Lay the jalapeno halves out on a large plate, ready to be topped. Place the milk in a small bowl and the flour in another small bowl. Place the breadcrumbs on a flat plate.

2. Place the cheddar cheese, bacon bits and cream cheese in a bowl and mix together. Spoon into the jalapeno halves. Dip the halves into the milk and then into the flour, coating them well. Set aside for 15-20 minutes.

3. Dip into the milk again and then coat with the breadcrumbs. Set aside for 15-20 minutes and then repeat. Set aside for another 15-20 minutes to dry.

4. Heat the oil in a large, deep frying pan to 180C/350F/Gas mark 4 and carefully drop in the jalapenos. Fry for 2-3 minutes each, until golden. Remove with a slotted spoon and drain on kitchen paper towel. Transfer to a serving dish and serve.

Mini Cheese & Tomato Pizzas (Serves 10-12)

Ingredients

4 large pizza bases
6-8 tbsps tomato puree
300g/3 cups of mozzarella cheese (grated)
300g/1 1/2 cups of tomatoes (sliced)

Method

1. Preheat the oven to 200C/400F/Gas mark 6. Using a 5cm pastry cutter,

ut out 10-12 rounds from the pizza bases and then spread tomato puree
ver each of them.

. Sprinkle with mozzarella cheese cover with the tomato slices and place in
he oven for 5-8 minutes.

*ip: For a fun party, let the kids choose their individual toppings and let them
ecorate the tops of their pizzas, making faces or patterns.*

arty Pretzels (Makes 40-45)

ngredients
45g/3 cups of plain flour
25ml/1 cup of milk (lukewarm)
 tbsps butter
egg (lightly beaten)
tbsp fresh yeast (crumbled)
tbsp caraway seeds
2 tsp sugar
2 tsp salt
 tsps coarse sea salt

Method
Place the yeast and sugar in a bowl; mash together. Add 4 tablespoons of
ilk and cream together into a paste-like consistency. Leave to one side in
 warm place for 20 minutes.

. Place the remaining milk and butter in a saucepan and gently heat, until
he butter has melted. Remove from the heat and leave to cool until
ukewarm.

. Sift the salt and the flour into a bowl, adding 2 teaspoons of caraway
eeds; stir together. Make a well in the centre and pour in the milk/butter
ixture. Gradually mix the flour with the liquid, working it into a dough.

. Sprinkle flour onto a clean work surface and turn out the dough. Knead
he dough for 8-10 minutes, until smooth. Mould the dough into a large ball
nd place it in a well greased bowl. Cover and place in a warm place for
0-45 minutes, until risen a little.

Party Pretzels/cont.

5. Sprinkle more flour over your work surface and turn out the dough. Knead the dough for 4-5 minutes and then split into two. Roll each piece into a long roll, (about 30cm), and cut into equally sized pieces, shaping each into a thin sausage shape, (about 14cm long).

6. Preheat the oven to 190C/375F/Gas mark 5. Grease 3-4 baking trays. Place each of the individual dough strips on the work surface and bend both ends towards you. Cross the loop about halfway along each side and then twist. Gently bend both ends back and press on top of the curve.

7. Pour boiling water into a saucepan, to about half full. Bring to the boil and add some of the dough to the water. Cook for 1 minute, until the dough pieces rise to the surface and remove. Repeat this process for all the dough pieces, draining them in a colander.

8. Place the dough pieces on the baking sheets and brush each with egg. Sprinkle the remaining caraway seeds evenly over the tops and place in the oven for 12-15 minutes, until golden brown. Remove from the oven and leave to cool. Sprinkle with sea salt and serve.

Smoked Salmon & Cream Cheese Rotollos (Makes 36 bites)

Ingredients

450g/2 cups of cream cheese
360g/3/4 lb smoked salmon
2 tbsps dill (chopped)
1/2 tbsps fresh lemon juice
6 flour tortillas (large)
1/2 tsp black pepper

Method

1. Place the cream cheese, dill, black pepper and lemon juice in a bowl and mix together.

2. Spread the mixture over the top of each of the tortillas and then cover with the smoked salmon. Roll the tortillas up firmly, in the style of a Swiss roll and trim each end, making them equal lengths.

3. Wrap the rolls in cling wrap, securing the ends. Refrigerate for between 1-2 hours, or until ready to use. To serve, slice diagonally into finger-food-sized pieces. Serve with rocket and cherry tomatoes.

Spicy Pecan Bites

Ingredients

400g/4 cups of pecan halves
1/2 tsp hot pepper sauce
2 tsps cinnamon
4 tbsps butter
2 tsps powdered artificial sweetener
1 tsp salt

Method

1. Heat the butter in a large frying pan and add the hot pepper sauce. Swirl around the base, coating evenly.

2. Add the pecan halves and cook over a medium heat for 2-3 minutes, stirring occasionally. Begin to stir the pecans continuously, until they start to brown, (be careful not to burn them). Stir in the salt, cinnamon and sweetener and remove from the heat. Transfer the pecans immediately to a serving bowl. Serve when cooled enough to taste.

Christmas

Christmas Panetonne & Creamy Custard Pudding (Serves 4)

Ingredients
55ml/1/4 cup of double cream
280ml/1 1/4 cups of milk
30g/1/8 cup of unsalted butter (softened)
3 eggs (beaten)
8-10 thick slices of panetonne
55g/1/4 cup of Demerara sugar
pinch of nutmeg

Method
1. Preheat the oven to 180C/350F/Gas mark 4. Grease a 1.5 litre ovenproof baking dish with butter. Lay the slices of panetonne on the base of the baking dish.

2. Place the beaten eggs, cream, milk and half of the sugar in a large measuring jug and beat together. Pour over the layers of panetonne and leave to stand for 15-20 minutes. Sprinkle the top with the remaining sugar.

3. Take a deep, roasting tray and half fill with boiling water. Carefully transfer to the lowest shelf in the oven and place the baking dish inside the roasting tray, (making sure that the water doesn't spill into the dish!). Bake in the oven for 40-45 minutes, until golden. Sprinkle with nutmeg and serve.

Eggnog (Serves 4)

Ingredients
4 eggs
300ml/1 1/3 cups of milk
75ml/1/3 cup of dark rum
110ml/1/2 cup of brandy
4 dashes of sugar syrup
nutmeg (to sprinkle)

Method
1. Place the brandy, rum, sugar syrup and egg into a food processor. Blend and then strain into a saucepan.

. Pour in the milk and bring to a low simmer – do not boil. Sprinkle over a
tle nutmeg and serve hot.

uxury Christmas cake (Serves 12)
ngredients
25g/3 cups of mixed fruit
25g/1 cup of cut mixed peel
25g/1 cup of glace cherries (chopped)
5g/2/3 cup of dried prunes (chopped)
)0g/2/3 cup of ground almonds
60g/2 1/4 cups of self-raising flour
25g/1 cup of butter (softened)
large eggs
0g/1/2 cup of light muscovado sugar
50g/2/3 cup of dark muscovado sugar
0ml/1/2 cup of dark rum
0ml/1/2 cup of brandy
orange, zest and juice
tsps mixed spices
/2 tsp ground cloves

Method
Place all of the fruit in a large saucepan, along with the brandy, rum,
nixed spice, peel, cloves, orange juice and zest. Bring to the boil and
emove from the heat. Leave to cool and then spoon into a sealable
container. Place in the refrigerator for 2 days, stirring daily.

. Preheat the oven to 130C/250F/Gas mark 2. Line a 23cm round cake tin
vith a double layer of baking paper, with the lining coming up 5cm above
ne tin sides.

. Place the butter and sugars in a bowl and beat together until creamy.
Whisk in the eggs, one at a time – whisking well after each new addition.
Carefully fold in the flour and ground almonds.

. Place half of the marinated fruit in a food processor and blend until
)ureed. Add to the cake mix, stirring it in well, followed by the remaining
ruit. Once well combined, spoon into the cake tin.

Luxury Christmas cake/cont.

5. Secure a double layer of baking paper, around the outside of the tin, with string. Place in the oven for 1 1/2 hours. Remove from the oven and cover the top of the cake with foil. Return to the oven and cook for a further 1 1/4-1 1/2 hours, until cooked.

6. Remove from the oven and leave to cool completely. Turn the cake out from the tin, removing all the layers of baking paper. Wrap in a new sheet of baking paper and a double layer of foil. Store in a cool, dark place until needed and ready to ice.

Mulled Wine (Serves 4-6)

Ingredients
1 bottle of red wine
1/2 bottle of white wine
1 orange
2 1/2 tbsps demerara sugar
2 cinnamon sticks
1/4 tsp ground cloves
1 inch of fresh root ginger (peeled & thinly sliced)

Method
1. Using a vegetable peeler or sharp knife, remove the zest from the orange in strips, (leaving the pith still on the orange). Juice the orange and transfer the juice into a large saucepan.

2. Pour the red and white wine into the saucepan, followed by the ground cloves, sugar, orange zest, cinnamon sticks and ginger. Stir together well, dissolving the sugar.

3. Cover the saucepan and heat over a medium/high heat. Heat until hot, but not to boiling point. Reduce the heat and continue to heat for 1 to 1 1/2 hours.

4. Adjust the sweetness, if required and strain the liquid into a serving jug. Serve hot.

Pancake Day

Lemon Butter Pancakes (Makes 4)

Ingredients

100g/1/2 cup of plain flour
55g/1/4 cup of unsalted butter (softened)
150ml/2/3 cup of milk
1 large egg
1 tbsps unsalted butter (softened)
pinch of salt
45g/1/3 cup of icing sugar
1/2 lemon, zest and juice

Method

1. Sift the plain flour and salt into a bowl and mix together. Make a well in the centre. Crack the egg into a cup, (removing any broken shell), and pour into the well in the centre of the bowl. Whisk together well.

2. Gradually pour in the milk, whisking continuously, until smooth. Place to one side.

3. Place 50g of the butter, lemon zest and icing sugar in a bowl and beat together until fluffy. Place to one side. Stir 1 tablespoon of the softened butter into the pancake batter.

4. Heat 1 tablespoon of butter in a non-stick frying pan and ladle in a quarter of the batter. Swirl the batter around the pan, coating the base. Cook for 1-2 minutes, (medium heat), and then flip over to cook the other side.

5. Remove from the pan and transfer to a serving plate; keep warm. Repeat this process for the remaining batter.

6. Melt a small amount of the lemon butter in the frying pan, with a little of the lemon juice and toss a pancake in the heated butter. Fold in half and transfer to a serving plate. Repeat this process for the remaining pancakes. Serve immediately.

Halloween

Ghostly-Hand Halloween Punch (Makes 2 Litres)

Ingredients
500ml/2 1/4 cups of ginger ale
500ml/2 1/4 cups of fizzy orange
225ml/1 cup of blackcurrant squash
500ml/2 1/4 cups of water
fruit slices (orange, apple, lemon, etc)
ice

Method
1. Firstly make the frozen hand. Wash a disposable glove and fill with water. Seal the glove tightly with an elastic band and place in the freezer. Freeze until hard.

2. Place all of the drink ingredients in a large punch bowl and mix together. Add the fruit slices and keep cool.

3. Just before serving add a couple of handfuls of ice. Remove the glove from the frozen 'hand' and place in the punch bowl. Share and scare!

Halloween Spider's Web Cake (Serves 8-12)

Ingredients for cake
170g/1 1/2 cups of plain flour
290g/2 1/3 cups of caster sugar
300ml/1 1/3 cup of evaporated milk
70g/2 1/2oz plain cooking chocolate (broken into chunks)
110g/1/2 cup of butter
2 large eggs
2 tsps baking powder
1/2 tsp salt
1/4 tsp bicarbonate of soda

Ingredients for filling:
70g/2 1/2oz plain cooking chocolate (melted)
490g/2 1/3 cups of caster sugar
280g/1 1/4 cups of butter
170ml/3/4 cup of evaporated milk
2 tsps vanilla extract

Method for cake
1 Preheat the oven to 180C/350F/Gas mark 4. Grease 2 x 23cm sandwich
cake tins, (with removable bottoms).

2. Sift the baking powder, bicarbonate of soda, caster sugar, salt and flour
into a large mixing bowl and stir together. Add the evaporated milk and
butter. Using a handheld electric mixer beat the mixture together for 2
minutes. Add the eggs and beat for a further 2 minutes.

3. Transfer the mixture equally into the cake tins and spread the tops out
with a palette knife. Melt the chocolate in a bowl over a saucepan of
simmering water. Remove from over the saucepan and leave to cool a
little.

4. Drizzle the chocolate evenly, in a spiral, over each cake. Gently drag a
knife from the inside of the cake to the out edge, at even points around
the cake; effectively feathering the lines to make a spider's web pattern.

5. Place in the oven for 35-40 minutes. Leave to cool for 10-15 minutes then
remove from the tins. Place on a wire cooling rack to cool completely.

Method for filling
1. Melt the chocolate in a bowl over a saucepan of simmering water.
Remove from the heat and pour the chocolate into a large bowl.

2. Add the butter, caster sugar, vanilla and evaporated milk and beat with a
handheld electric mixer until smooth.

3. Warm a knife under hot water and spread the filling on the inside of the
cake halves; sandwich together. Ice the sides of the cake with the
remaining filling.

Celebrations

Easter

Easter Bunny Biscuits (Makes 12)

Ingredients
115g/1 cup of plain flour
30g/1/8 cup of butter (room temperature)
65g/1/2 cup of caster sugar
1 small egg
1/2 tbsp orange juice
3/4 tsp orange zest
1/8 tsp salt
3/4 tsp baking powder

Method
1. Preheat the oven to 190C/375F/Gas mark 5. Place the sugar and butter in a bowl and beat together until creamy. Add the egg and beat until the mixture is smooth. Gradually stir in the flour, followed by the salt and baking powder. Combine well. Mix in the orange zest and juice.

2. Lightly flour a clean work surface, roll out the dough using a rolling pin. Roll the dough into approximately a 6mm thickness.

3. Using a rabbit-shaped biscuit cutter, cut out 10-12 shapes. Place on a baking tray and bake in the oven for 8-10 minutes, until golden.

4. Remove from the oven and leave to cool on a wire cooling rack. Once cooled, ice and decorate as desired.

Hot Cross Buns (Makes 10-12)
NB. You will need a bread-making machine for this recipe.

Ingredients Buns
380g/3 1/3 cups of plain flour
150g/1 cup of dried currants
60g/1/2 cup of caster sugar
55g/1/4 cup of butter
170ml/3/4 cup of warm water
1 large egg
1 egg white

egg yolk

tbsp dried milk powder

tsp ground cinnamon

tbsp dried active baking yeast

inch of salt

tbsps water

ngredients Icing

0g/1/2 cup of icing sugar

tsps milk

'4 tsp vanilla extract

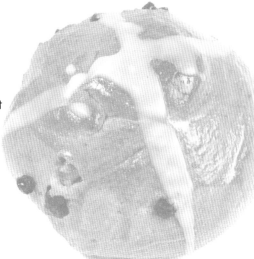

Method for buns

Grease a 22 x 33 cm baking tin. Place the yeast, flour, egg white, egg, warm water, butter, caster sugar, milk powder and salt in a bread-making machine and begin on a dough programme.

. About 5 minutes before the end of the programme, add the cinnamon and currants. When the programme has finished leave the dough in the machine, until the dough has doubled in size.

. Remove the dough from the machine onto a floured surface and punch down. Leave for 10-15 minutes.

. Shape the dough into 10-12 balls and place in the baking tin. Cover and eave in a warm place, for about 40-45 minutes, until the dough balls have doubled in size.

. Preheat the oven to 190C/375F/Gas mark 5. Place the egg yolk and 2 ablespoons of water in a small bowl and mix together. Brush over the top of the dough balls.

. Place in the oven for 20 minutes, until golden. Remove the buns from the in and place on a wire cooling rack to cool.

Method for icing

. Once the buns have cooled, place the vanilla, milk and icing sugar in a bowl and mix together. Brush a cross on each bun.

Bonfire Night

Bonfire-Cooked Food Parcels (Serves 4)

Ingredients

450g/1 lb chicken breast (diced)
250g/2 cups of mushrooms (sliced)
2 onions (chopped)
4 small potatoes (diced)
1 red pepper (deseeded & sliced)
1 yellow pepper (deseeded & sliced)
2 cloves of garlic (thinly sliced)
juice of 1 lemon
4 tbsps olive oil
8 square sheets of foil
4 rectangular sheets of foil

Method

1. Place all of the ingredients in a large bowl and mix together well. Leave for 10 minutes.

2. Equally divide the mixture between 4 of the foil sheets and top each with another sheet of foil. Secure the edges by wrapping them up tightly. Wrap each parcel with one of the rectangular sheets of foil.

3. Cook in the hot coals of a bonfire for 40-45 minutes, until the chicken is cooked through.

Bonfire Toffee

Ingredients

450g/1lb demerara sugar
30g/1/8 cup of butter
225ml/1 cup of water
2-3 tbsps golden syrup
1 tsp vinegar

Method

1. Butter a shallow baking tin. Place the water, vinegar and butter in a saucepan and add the syrup and sugar gradually, stirring over a gentle heat until the sugar has dissolved.

Celebrations

Bring to the boil and simmer for 25-30 minutes. Test that the toffee syrup ready by dripping a few drops into cold water – when the drops arden-up the toffee is ready.

Transfer to the baking tin and leave to set. When partially set, mark the ab of toffee into pieces with a knife. Once set, break out of the tin.

ot Bonfire Night Punch (Serves 4-6)

ngredients

25ml/2 1/3 cups of apple juice
00ml/1 1/3 cup of light rum
0g/1/2 cup of light brown sugar
litre of water
cinnamon sticks
orange spice tea bags

Method

Pour the water into a large saucepan and bring to the boil. Remove from ne heat and add the tea bags. Cover and leave for 4-5 minutes.

Remove the tea bags and add the apple juice, rum, sugar and cinnamon sticks. Return to the heat and heat until hot, but not boiling.

adle the punch into mugs and serve hot.

offee Apples (Makes 6)

ngredients

crunchy apples (washed & dried, stalks removed)
20g/2 3/4cups of demerara sugar
0g/1/2 cup of unsalted butter
0ml/1/2 cup of water
tbsps caster sugar
tsps vanilla essence
tsps vinegar
owl of cold water
ugar

Toffee Apples/cont.

Method

1. Push a lollipop stick into each of the apples, making sure that they are secured well. Sprinkle a baking tray with sugar.

2. Place the other ingredients in a saucepan and bring to the boil. Simmer for 25-30 minutes. Test that the toffee syrup is ready by dripping a few drops into cold water – when the drops harden-up the toffee is ready.

3. Remove from the heat and dip each apple into the toffee. Take each ou and cool in the air for 3-4 seconds, before putting the apple back into the toffee to ensure that the apple is thickly coated.

4. Dip each coated apple into cold water and place, lollipop stick-up, onto the baking tray. Leave to set.

Index

index

Index